# BLESSINGS IN DISGUISE

Dr. Brenda Craven, PhD

ISBN 978-1-312-35905-5

# Forward

Domestic violence runs rampant in today's society. Most goes unreported due to fear or shame. But for those that are reported, the journey is long and hard for the victim…emotionally, spiritually, and physically. The memories, flashbacks, and nightmares are very real. But it can be overcome. Trust is hard to come by, but you will learn to trust again. It is with great pleasure that I am able to share this book with you…my struggles, pain, deepest thoughts, despair, joy and jubilance. With the strength and grace of God, I was able to find my identity and self-worth again, and accomplish what God planned for me. It is my greatest prayer that this book will reach, help, and uplift someone who is going through domestic violence. You are who God says you are; you are beautiful, you are precious, and you are a priceless gem that God felt was worth the life of his son. So find your footing again and begin to walk on the road and path that God has placed you on…it's your destiny.                    –Dr. Brenda Craven

*I would highly recommend this book to help you get through life's struggles, and not to ever give up.  Brenda stayed with God and showed a wonderful ability to stand and stay the course…not give up and run.  This book will give you the courage to face life's battles and come out a winner.*

*Dr. Zalmer Nichols, Th.D., PhD*

*Chancellor, Faith Bible College*

*The story of Domestic Violence is not easy to tell, especially when the story is your own.  Blessings in Disguise tells this story honestly and shows how even the strongest individuals can struggle with issues of violence for years.  We here are at Rose Brooks Center are incredibly grateful for individuals, like Dr. Brenda Craven, who are willing to share their stories, so that others can learn from their life experiences.  She has endured so much heartbreak, fear, and loneliness, yet she has risen above it and has used these experiences to help women who are dealing with many of the issues she has faced and overcome.  We are so proud of everything Brenda has accomplished and for the small part we played in her success."*

*Sharla K. Nolte*

*Manager of Marketing and Donor Communications*

*Rose Brooks Center*

"Therefore if any man be in Christ, he is a new creature: old things are passed away; behold all things are become new." II Cor. 5:17

Brenda's story is an example of II Corinthians 5:17. She allows us to see her 'becoming process' as she is being formed into the image of her Savior. She shows the pain, suffering, and trials of her journey with an honest revealing of her heart and its responses to each new challenge without excusing decisions she made in that process.

Brenda is buffeted by her life circumstances, always willing to love, always willing to forgive, while she is not aware of the molding, and remolding of the potter who is at work making and remaking her into the vessel through which HE can flow. She deals with her own temptations with forthright honest telling as she unlocks the many rooms of her heart where her memories are stored.

A phrase in Galatians 5:6 tells us that 'faith worketh by love." Brenda's story shows the reader that circumstances don't dictate the presence or absence of love, but that faith is always at work where love is, because that is God's presence.

Brenda was a student in a writing class I was privileged to teach; but Brenda is my friend, my sister in the Lord, but even more, she is connected to my own heart as my family. As her story unfolded, I could see reflections to my own heart, with hurts, and the search for healing and love. I could see the person of our heavenly Father, His identity being LOVE, with the knowledge that true healing is actually His love kissing all the boo boos in our lives and making us whole.

It is with loving admiration of my sister in Christ that I not only recommend this book, but I can see our Father's own endorsement on the ministry it represents.

Dr. Margaret Hayden, PhD

Christian Journalism

## Chapter 1 – The Beginning

"Life isn't all it's cut out to be," my mother used to say.  You climb

mountains, you swim oceans, you cross valleys you don't want to cross, but the

real accomplishment comes when you conquer them.  My mother was a very wise

woman, but she was also a woman who believed in going through undue stress

and torment to keep the family together.

At the age of 36, she met a man at Union Station in Omaha, Nebraska.  He

was a good-looking 46 year old man who was a chef.  My mom had several

professions, but the one she loved and cherished the most was being a

professional entertainer who sang and played piano.  She was traveling through

after a "gig" when their eyes fixated on each other.  That was all it took.  They

were soon married and rented a small house in Omaha on Erskine Street, and

before long, I was on the way.  Mom always told me about how Dad purchased

this German Shepard that they named Tony, and this dog turned out to be the

best guard dog in the world.  He would patrol from one end of the house to

another (the doors could be left wide open), and I even heard stories of how he would pick up my baby bottle when I dropped it out of my crib, take it into the bedroom, and wake up my mom to alert her. Dad fed the dog from a fork (which according to him, made the dog meaner), and at times the dog would not let my mom in the house when she came home from working because he was protecting the house...thanks to Dad. But, there was also a darker side of the story. It seems that Dad, in fits of anger would hit her and verbally abuse her...all the time while she was pregnant with me. Really? The father that helped to create me would do something to harm me before I even arrived here?

Mom said she continued to work as an entertainer all the way up to when she went into labor. Her drink of choice while she worked...I.W. Harper Whiskey and beer. (It's alright folks...I turned out well...besides I'm writing this story right?) This would have been a glorious occasion except for the fact that I was arriving way too early...a month and a half early. She always talked about the hours she spent in labor to deliver this little 3 pound 6 ounce bundle which was smaller than a loaf of bread. I remained in what used to be Doctor's Hospital in Omaha, NE for 45 days in an incubator until I was strong enough to go home, but according to Mom, the I. W. Harper seemed to have aided me in being as physically strong as I was as a "preemie." Being too small to buy clothes for, my mom would either make them or purchase doll clothes to place on me. I can't even imagine to this day wearing doll clothes as a baby!

2 years later, the Musician's Local Union sent my mom to Colorado to perform. She packed me (2 years old) up in the car, and she, dad, and I took the long trip to La Junta, Colorado. This was supposed to be a few night's venture, but it turned out to be permanent. Dad had stomach ulcers that had started to bleed, and was too sick to make the trip back, so the decision was made to settle in La Junta and we made that our home. I was too young to remember any of it, but from what mom said, it was one heck of a situation.

## Chapter 2 – Curiosity

I can remember living in that little house on Lewis Street…it was painted pink and it had shutters on the windows. Next door lived the Ponces, a Hispanic family who welcomed us into the neighborhood with open arms and provided us with an endless supply of homemade tortillas. We had moved into a community where there really wasn't very many people of African-American ethnicity, so at Christmas time, when I opened one of my presents which was an African American doll, I did not want her. Not that I didn't like black people, there just weren't enough of them for me to relate to as a small child (Mom humorously claimed that issue arose due to the fact that all I saw for the first 45 days of my life was white…doctor's coats and nurse uniforms.) But, I soon warmed up to my doll and named her "Maudine," after one of our neighbors across the street who happened to be black.

I had my first experience with the Holy Spirit at a Baptist Church in La Junta. Maudine and her sister Melodine attended this church and asked my mother if they could take me along for Sunday school. I remember the little card they gave me with the picture of Jesus holding a lamb, and the scripture on the back...I am the good shepherd, the good shepherd giveth his life for the sheep (John 10:11). That was one of the first bible verses I learned as a child. As we went into service, I remember seeing ladies dressed in white, jumping around, hollering, crying, and then falling out on the floor. Being a child, 3 years of age, there is only one scary assumption for me...she fell, she's not moving......SHE'S DEAD! I began to cry and it took several of the women in the church to get me calmed down, and eventually someone had to bring me back home to mom. Of course when I got home, I had to try and tell her what happened with my limited vocabulary, but she definitely understood when I said someone died. She immediately started laughing and couldn't stop. "Why would my mom laugh about somebody falling and getting hurt?" I couldn't understand that. But mom, in all her wisdom, said "She didn't die...she just got happy and fainted. The woman is ok." "Got Happy." Now that's a term I haven't heard for a while.

Then came the night that Dad got really, really sick. I was nearly 4 years old at the time. It seemed that he kept vomiting all over everything and it wasn't stopping. Then mom managed to get him into the bathroom and sit him on the toilet. I didn't understand until I was older what was really happening. Dad's ulcers had begun to bleed again, and this time it was bad. I remember mom continually running back and forth to get buckets for dad to vomit in. At one point, I saw her sit down and start to cry, so I went over to her to see what was wrong and she pushed me away. As she sat quietly, she said, "Daddy is very sick and I'm trying to help him. Mommy's ok." She then went back to running back and forth with buckets for Dad. After about 30 minutes of this, one of the next door neighbors came over and helped her get Dad out of the house and into a car. Mrs. Ponce took me home with her, and as she sat me on her lap, she said, "Your daddy is going to the hospital." It wasn't until much later that I realized the extent of my Dad's sickness. He had duodenal ulcers that had ruptured and he was hemorrhaging internally. What he was vomiting up was blood and he was also passing it through his bowels. He had to have part of his intestines cut out, and according to the doctors, if my mom would have waited until morning to get help, Dad would have died. It took him quite a while to recover, but at least I still had him.

Not long after that, it was Mom's turn. Dad took Mom to the hospital, and once again, I was left with the Ponces. He came back without Mom, and it was a few days later that he placed me in our 1966 Chrysler Imperial, turned around, and excitedly said, "I have a surprise for you!" As the car slowly moved down the snow covered streets, I looked at the sunlight shining through the bare trees, and wondered what this surprise could be. The car stopped in the parking lot of the hospital, and I was left alone there in my excitement. My imaginations went wild..."Is it a puppy? No, wait, it's Mommy, I haven't seen her...maybe mommy is coming home." I wiggled impatiently in my seat as Dad slowly walked into the hospital. After a few minutes of sitting with my eyes firmly fixed on the hospital door, out walked Mom and Dad, but I noticed that mom was holding something in her arms...something in a blue blanket. As she sat down in the car, I leaned over the seat and asked, "What are you holding, mommy?" She opened up the blanket and said, "This is your new baby brother." Even now, I don't even remember mom being pregnant, I don't remember her stomach being big, but there are lots of pictures showing her pregnant with my brother whom she named after our dad. To keep confusion down, we just called him Junior

I was as curious as a child could be, always getting into things and putting things into my mouth that I shouldn't. If there could have been a piggy bank made out of me, they would have had quite a savings. Such things as plastic fruit, which were placed everywhere for decoration, were prime targets for me. Spankings were inevitable for me, as I always chewed all the plastic grapes that were in the bowls on the dining room table. But one particular time, that nasty habit of placing things in my mouth threatened my very life. Mom was performing at a club a few blocks away, and Dad was watching my brother and me…at least he was supposed to be. He had fallen asleep on the couch, and I, being the curious child went on a venture. On the floor next to the washer was a bottle of Clorox. I had watched Mom pour it into a cup numerous times and pour it into the washer with the clothes. At that time, Clorox had no color, it was clear just like water. So, naturally, I assumed it was water. In my curiosity, I unscrewed the cap and was able to pour a little in the cup and drink it. Immediately I felt this extreme burning sensation in my throat, stomach, and nose, and ran to wake up my Dad. I shook him and he immediately jumped, then sat up and asked "What's wrong?" "I drank rox," I cried out as my little eyes, nose, throat, and stomach felt like they were on fire. Dad thought I had swallowed rocks, so he picked me up, turned me upside down, and proceeded to hit me on the back to get me to cough up the rocks. I kept screaming, "No Daddy….I drank rox!" "Show me what you're talking about," he firmly said, and I took him by the hand and pointed. Dad never moved as fast as he did that night! It was very late at night, around 10:00pm, but he placed my brother and me in the car, drove a few blocks away and interrupted Mom who was in the middle of performing and rushed me to the hospital. The doctors tried in every way to get me to drink large masses of milk. I drank the first glass, but refused the second. I was not feeling well at all, and couldn't understand why my insides were burning. I fought, screamed and hollered, with all my might...I just wanted the burning to go away. Finally, the doctors had to restrain me (at 4 years old...mind you) and pump my stomach. It was a terrible feeling to experience them placing the tubes up my nose and telling me to swallow. I could feel them going down the back of my throat. Needless to say, Mom definitely moved the bleach to a higher location where I couldn't reach it.

I admit it, if I didn't like something, everyone knew I didn't like it. My first dentist visit was a disaster, and I gave the dentist the fight of his life...putting his fingers in my mouth, trying to put these weird foreign looking instruments in, and to top it off, turning on this extremely bright light and shining it in my face. Nope, I was not a happy camper...he knew it, the dentist office knew it, and when the family friend that offered to take me to the dentist brought me back home, Dad knew it. He pretty much let me know that he didn't like what I did by administering a whipping on me that had an adverse effect on me for years. In matter of fact, until about a year ago, I had a fear of dentists and refused to go to them until I had an issue that arose that required immediate assistance (can anyone say Root Canal?) Yep, I associated that whipping with going to the dentist and I had a major hatred for them, which now has been removed. Thank you Lord. So much more was yet to come, and there would be so much more that I would be delivered from.  Little did I know, just how much everything would

change my life.

## Chapter 3 – The Pain Begins

After living in La Junta for around 3 years, my parents made the decision to move 11 miles west to Rocky Ford, which was a small farming community.  Mom and Dad still worked in La Junta though; Dad as a chef at the Kit Carson Hotel and Restaurant, and Mom as an administrator with the Head Start Programs.  Of course she still entertained in the evenings at times.  That meant new schools, new friends, and new acquaintances, which for me, was rather difficult, seeing that there were not very many black families within a 50 mile radius.  In matter of fact, there was only one other black family in Rocky Ford at the time besides us.  You can imagine how rude and disrespectful some people were, and that rudeness trickled down through the children.  Kindergarten wasn't a problem for me, but once I began first grade, that's when the "N" word came into play.  I came home many a day crying because of it, and Dad finally got tired of it and taught me how to fight because no efforts that he or mom were making were working. But one day, Dad came home with something that made me forget about all that…he came home with a dog.  We had another dog earlier which was named Tramp, but he had died.  So someone at Dad's job had given this little brown Chihuahua to him.  He was cutest little thing…with pointy ears, a long nose, and a short little tail.  But, many were fooled by this small little creature,

who at one time, made a Doberman retreat.   Dad didn't have to pay for the dog,

so he named him Charger.  Charger became my best friend, and both my brother

and I became very fond of him.

Not long after the move, Dad was fired from his job and began to drink

heavily.  The reason why is unclear, but I know he was unhappy, and his temper

flared up more frequently.  One day, I did something wrong, and he was going to

beat me, but, I was determined that he was going to have to catch me first.  So,

out of the house I ran, with him chasing me…hollering and swearing at me the

whole time (I was about 7 years old then, so I was pretty quick).   Junior, who was

3 at the time, was walking as well, so he had quite a challenge on his hands.  I

kept running around the house as fast as I could to keep Dad from catching me.

At one point, he tried the "stop and wait" tactic to catch me as I continued to run

the same direction around the house.  I figured he would be doing that, so I quit

running and sat on the front porch for a little while.  By this time, he was so angry

and frustrated with me, he angrily said, "I will tear your butt up once I catch you."

Of course, I made sure that wouldn't happen that day.  Soon it was time for him

to pick up Mom from work, and I knew if Mom were home, he could not get out

of hand with the whipping, so I stayed out of his reach.  He placed my brother in the car with him and left me home by myself until they came back. Of course, the beating never happened.

Then came the day when I either talked back to him, lied to him, or something. But, whatever it was, it made Dad very upset. So upset that he slapped me across the face so hard that it left his hand print in the right side of my face. It actually was bleeding and bruised. Our neighbors across the street, who became our extended family, happened to see my face and called my Mom on her job to let her know. She was enraged when she saw my face, and angrily commanded Dad saying, "All discipline from this time forward will be administered by me. If you can't spank them on the spot that God has created for that, you have no business placing your hands on the children at all!" That redirected his rage towards her now, and she had to shift her energy from protecting us to protecting herself.

There is one situation that sticks out in my mind even today. It's one that I struggled with for years until I really had the nerve to speak to a girl that was a good friend of mine and apologize to her about it. I was in the 4th grade, and the school I attended was about 15 minutes walking distance away from home. My friend, who I will just call Jessie, lived a couple blocks away from the school. So, every day we'd walk home together, and Dad always knew when to expect me home...he had everything timed to the second. One day, Jessie and I decided to stop at this little area close to the school that had a pile of rock salt. Kids always used to stop there, pick up some rock salt and eat it (wonder how many of us suffer from high blood pressure now.) Anyhow, that made me a little late getting home from school. Of course dad was waiting on me when I walked through the door and wanted an explanation. I told him the truth and he did not believe me. He looked at my face and said, "Your eyes look glassy. You have taken something and I want to know who gave you the drugs to take." I cried, pleaded and swore that nobody had given me anything, but dad said, "If you don't tell me the truth, I will beat you until you do." So, I had to come up with a story to appease him. I told him that Jessie had given me these pills to take and that she said they would make me feel good. Of course he asked for size and color. Once I finished the story, he decided that he needed to call the chief of police, have him come over, and I was to repeat this story to him word for word. Can you imagine a nine year old having to tell a lie to their parents and having to remember everything you said and repeat it to the police with your parents monitoring every word? But I did just that. Through my tears, I repeated the lie to the chief of police that I was forced to tell my dad. Of course he said he would check into the situation, but I later found out from my mom that the chief had talked to her and expressed that

he knew that it was a lie, but also knew that I was scared to death of my dad.

Both my brother and I laid in bed many nights listening to mom and dad arguing

and fighting.  Sometimes dad hit mom, sometimes he said nasty, evil things to her

and she just cried and wouldn't fight back.  But we didn't know just how bad it

would get.

## Chapter 4 – The Big Move

We had the greatest neighbors in Rocky Ford. One family in particular was like extended family to us. The parents would get together constantly to play a friendly hand of bid wiz or spades, while the kids made their own fun. Most of our fun came from standing in front of the television set and trying to cover up the scantily dressed women on "Hee-Haw" from the males in the house. We would play hide and seek or kick the bucket. It was nothing to have the whole neighborhood of kids in on the action. But, one of our favorite things was to run behind the mosquito sprayer when it would drive by leaving a thick white smelly fog. There were irrigation ditches running everywhere throughout the town which were usually filled with water...hence the mosquito problem. We would wait, then run behind the truck in the midst of the fog, laughing at those unfortunate ones who happened to run into a parked car or two. Of course we never took into consideration the effect that breathing in those chemicals would have on our health. Some of us have passed on, and I can't help but wonder if our escapade was responsible in some way.

The parents watched each other's kids, and unlike today, disciplined each other's kids. We had grown so close to each other, so when it was decided that we were moving a couple miles outside of town, it was a little difficult. We still

had the get togethers, they were just a little less frequent. Mom and Dad had

decided to purchase a two bedroom mobile home and placed it in a trailer court 2

miles east of town. It was a nice place though...the bedrooms were at opposite

ends of the trailer with the living room and kitchen/dining room in the center, and

a decent sized bathroom was right next to Junior's and my bedroom. We had to

share a bedroom, which really wasn't so cool once we became teenagers. We

later purchased a washer and placed it in the bathroom as well. How did we dry

the clothes? Mom strung a clothesline inside the trailer from one end to another

and just hung clothes on it with clothes pins. We didn't have much, but we made

it work.

Dad had begun to drink a lot more by this time. It was nothing for him to

get a case of beer in the morning and be ready for another case by that evening.

It had gotten to the point that he had driven into town drunk to get more beer

and had an accident. There was snow on the ground, so that didn't help either.

Drunk driving laws weren't so strict back then, so he just got a slap on the hand.

When his car didn't work, he would walk 2 miles into town to get his beer and

carry it 2 miles back home. Mom worked very hard to support us and keep food

on the table, while Dad drank it up. I think at one point, Dad took out a 2nd mortgage on the trailer without Mom knowing about it to have more beer money. It upset her, but yet she stayed with him. The fights got worse...Junior and I would wake up at 2:00 in the morning to Mom crying and screaming at Dad, and Dad threatening to beat her to a pulp. We would open our bedroom door and come out, and Mom would look up, dry her tears and say, "It's ok, go back to bed." Dad, on the other hand, would continue to call her every name he could possibly think of, while accusing her of being unfaithful and sleeping with whatever black male came through town. There were times that we would wake up the next morning to see Mom with a black eye, a fat lip, or bruises, but she always managed to cover them up and come up with some lame excuse for the injury.

The trailer court sat right next to a gravel pit which belonged to a concrete company which was about ¼ mile down the road. As gravel was dug out, it created a natural pond which in the summertime, we would sneak down and play in, against warnings of it being dangerous. We would jump in and swim, praying our parents never discovered what we were doing. The winters were brutal at times. It was nothing to get a couple feet of snow, and we always had to go to school. We very seldom had school shut down because of snow. We may have had to walk through hip deep snow to get to our bus stop, but the roads were clear enough for the buses to get us there. Summers were very hot, and when severe weather hit, it was pretty scary…especially when there were high winds. Even though our trailer was anchored into a concrete slab, we could still see the walls inside move as if they were breathing. I remember once looking out a window when the wind was very high and seeing a trailer not far from ours flip over. We went to school with the kids who lived there, and luckily, nobody was critically injured.

One year, when I was about 9 years old, Mom, Junior, and I received the opportunity of a lifetime. We were asked to be in a stage production of the musical "Showboat" which was being put together by the Picketwire Players in La Junta. Mom, being an entertainer, played the part of "Queenie", which meant she sang quite a bit in the show. She wasn't the main character, but she loved the part she had. Junior played a clown, and I played one of several slave girls who sang a couple of songs and danced a little. I remember long rehearsals and performing over and over again. There were wardrobe changes…going on stage for a couple minutes, running back off, changing clothes, then going back on stage. Then there was the extensive time it took to get my makeup done, then the quick removal of it at the end of the show with cold cream and cotton balls. I really did not like the process at all, but at the end of the show, when each group of performers would run center stage and take a bow, the whole auditorium

thundered with the applause and shouts from the audience.  Flashes of light from

the cameras of the newspaper critics and columnists lit up the room, and it was a

feeling that I would never forget.  Even my 4th grade teacher, Mrs. Craig, came to

see the show, and told me how proud she was of me.  A picture of my Mom,

Junior, and I in costume, appeared in the Rocky Ford Daily Gazette along with

another black family who also was in the play.  I can't recall the family's name, but

I know that the father played the singing character opposite my mom, the mother

and daughter along with me completed the group of the slave girls who sang and

danced, and their son was a clown just like my brother.  Of course this

mountaintop experience was short lived as my father saw the picture in the

paper.  The accusations began...Mom was sleeping with her co-star (even though

we told him over and over again the other woman in the picture was his wife).

Then came the racism statements... "White people were putting on a play, and

the black people, as usual, were cast as slaves and jokers."  He made it very clear

that we were allowing ourselves to be made fools of and he was embarrassed and

angry about it.  Our sense of accomplishment and pride was now being attacked

and crushed by Dad's disapproval.  It was so bad that anytime someone drove

down the highway past the trailer court and honked, no matter who or what they were honking for, Dad said it was someone honking for mom and started with the verbal and sometimes physical abuse.  Junior was involved with plays later on in his high school years, but I never involved myself with them again, and we never did another play together.

Chapter 5 – The Loaded Gun

It was the summer of 1979 and I had just finished my freshman year of high school. Junior had just finished 5th grade. I was 15 years old and Junior was 11. Dad had secured a job at Rocky Ford High School as a custodian. This was not a happy moment for me, as his presence was ruining any chance of me getting a date with anyone. Nobody wanted to ask me out because they feared my father. One instance, a boy that I had the biggest crush on asked if I needed a ride home after a track meet. I was so excited that he asked and wanted to accept his offer, but Dad had already left the house to come and pick me up and there was no way to contact him. That opportunity was lost, never to present itself again.

This particular summer was a hotter than usual one. There hadn't been a day in which the temperature was below 100 degrees for about a 2 week stretch. We had an air conditioner that worked, but it was an old one that cooled with water. Every so often, we'd have to go outside, take the side of the air conditioner off, turn on the water hose, and fill the bottom of it up with water. Then we would wet all four sides of it down. Each side contained a filter to keep dirt and dust from blowing into the trailer. Once it was filled with water, a pump would turn on in the air conditioner and pump water to keep all the filters soaked...this generated cooler air.  If the water ran out and the filters dried up, it would only blow hot air.  This was an ancient piece of equipment, but it did the job.

Dad as usual was doing his normal thing...drinking.  I don't recall what started it, but a fight broke out between him and Mom.  It was escalating quickly, and Junior and I weren't sure how this would end up.  I don't even remember what the fight was about, but Dad was sitting on one side of the kitchen table and Mom on the other.  He was so upset that he stood up, walked into the bedroom, and then walked back out holding a pistol in his hand.  He proceeded to sit down at the table, then laid the pistol down and proceeded to address my mom saying, "Now, tell me one more lie...I'll blow your head off.  Open your mouth again!"  Mom sat there crying, and I could see the fear in her face and in her eyes.  He loaded the gun with bullets in our sight to prove he wasn't playing.  I immediately grabbed the phone and said, "Put the gun down or I'm calling the Sheriff."  Of course, talking to a drunk person is like talking to a brick wall.  Mom was pleading with me to set the phone down and not call, but I was not playing either.  Dad began talking about Junior and me saying, "They aren't even my kids...they don't even have my blood type."  He had a very rare one, so it was no surprise that neither one of us had his.  I had taken a biology class my freshman year, and one of the subjects was genetics, so I was quick to begin refuting his comments.  I'm not sure what happened, but my freshman year, I had 7 classes and h 1 straight A's with the exception of Biology in which I had a D. I don't think Mom and Dad ever was able to get an answer as to why this was the only class I failed in, but I ended up changing classes in the middle of the school year. Dad was quick to point out that I was lecturing him on something I couldn't even pass a class on. That was a low blow on his part, but I still stood my ground. He couldn't refute the birthmark on the upper right side of my chest that he also bore in the same place, or the mole located on the middle of the inside of my left arm, which he bore also on the same arm and in the same location. Mom kept saying, "Be quiet," but I wasn't about to be silent...Dad still had the gun in his hand. Mom began to cry and say, "I haven't done anything wrong," and Dad cocked the pistol to shoot. I picked up the phone again, and once again Mom said, "Put it down!" Junior had been trying to leave the house, and Mom had stopped him from leaving the whole time. But, once Dad cocked the gun, there was no stopping him. With a tank top and shorts on, and no shoes, Junior ran out into the 100+ degree weather, down our metal steps that I'm sure were heated way beyond the actual temperature, ½ mile down the hot asphalt road to a neighbor's house to call the sheriff. Dad was livid now. About 15 minutes later, the sheriff drove up with Junior in the car. As I started to run out of the house to meet the sheriff, mom blocked me and told me to be quiet. As the sheriff let Junior out of the car, he asked, "Is there a problem here?" Mom coaxed Junior into the trailer and calmly said, "No. There's been a little misunderstanding, but everything is alright now." Dad was still sitting at the table, but had laid the loaded pistol down on it. I was steadily trying to push and get past Mom to tell him the truth, and she was preventing me from doing it. Junior was in tears as he walked back into the trailer, his poor little feet full of blisters from running on the hot asphalt to get help for mom. Did this not matter to anyone at all? The sheriff asked one more time, "Are you sure everything is alright?" Mom said, "Yes." As the sheriff drove away, both my brother and I couldn't help but to feel a sense of failure in protecting someone very important to us, and that there was no end to this madness. Why wouldn't Mom talk to the sheriff? Why wouldn't she tell him that Dad was threatening her with a loaded pistol? Why wouldn't she tell him about all the beatings she had taken? Why didn't the sheriff sense something and proceed to check the situation out? But most of all, why was she protecting this man? I had seriously premeditated about removing this curse from my mom. I had laid in bed late at night thinking about ways to kill Dad in his sleep, or even while he was awake for that matter. I just didn't want Mom to be hurt any more. But, then I thought about what Mom would go through with a daughter in prison for killing her father. I thought about having to deal with that reality for the rest of my life, and it wasn't worth the effort, but it still brought me peace, in a strange kind of way, to know that it was possible.

We were always told to keep what happened in the family within the four walls. We weren't to tell friends, teachers, members of our church, or even other family members. But, our grades were starting to suffer, and I couldn't deal with the pressure of it all anymore, so I confided in some people from church, and even my best friend, who is still my best friend to this day. It did not make Mom or Dad happy at all, but I did not care. The tide was about to change, and I wanted my feet to be the first to feel the breaking of the waves as it did.

32

## Chapter 6 – The Scare

As a teenager, I was still the prankster.  If I wanted to get out of something, I would try to get Mom to believe something was wrong with me.  Mom was very wise and figured me out every single time.  So, I had a very high failure rate when it came to lying to her about things.

One Sunday morning, I woke up and decided that I did not want to go to church that day.  So I came up with a scheme to fake being sick.  I planned this very well.  Mom came in to wake me up, and I immediately went into "I'm really sick" mode.  At first she did not believe me, then somehow, I was able to get the tears to start.  To this day, I don't know how that happened, but it sure helped the drama factor.  I told her, in my most pitiful voice, "My stomach hurts so badly and I can't move."  She asked, "Can you walk?"  I started crying harder as if in severe pain and said, "No."  I couldn't have planned what happened next in a million years.  Mom called the ambulance to come and get me.  I really did not want to go to church, and I wasn't going to give in.  Wow, a free ambulance ride to the hospital 11 miles away, with sirens blaring...how cool was that?  I'd get there, they'd examine me and find nothing wrong.  By then, it would be too late to go to church...mission accomplished.  I moaned and groaned the whole way to the hospital, sticking to my complaints of abdominal pain. By the time we reached the emergency room, I was living it up. I was going to let this play out for a little while longer, then I could go home and sleep for the rest of the day. The emergency room doctors talked to me and mom for a minute, asked us a few questions, then decided they needed to run a few tests. I thought I was home free until they came back and told Mom, "We need to hospitalize her." Whoa, wait a minute…did they actually figure out that I was lying and decide to teach me a lesson? I felt great, never felt greater in my life. I was a little fatigued, but figured it was nothing that a day of being lazy couldn't fix. The doctors told Mom, "She has mononucleosis and needs to be admitted immediately." It was the non-contagious type.  Ok…game over. I pleaded with Mom to take me home, but she wasn't listening. As they rolled me into the hospital room, and changed me into a hospital gown, I was really beginning to get scared. Mom was trying to console me, but it wasn't helping. Finally, I decided to go along with the flow. If they'd caught onto me, I'd play along but they weren't going to beat me at my game. 12 hours later, I wasn't playing the game anymore. I was so sick. I was running a fever well over 100 degrees, and felt like something had completely zapped every bit of strength I had. I began coughing and couldn't stop, and felt very congested. I was taking pill after pill after pill, and just as I was dropping into a deep sleep, some nurse who didn't know how to draw blood would come in and wake me up to draw it. So much blood had been drawn out of my left arm that they couldn't find a good vein to draw from anymore, so I suggested using my right arm. I was in the hospital for a total of 5 days which scared more people than just me and Mom.

The prior week, I had been in basketball practice and saw one of my teammates collapse during warm ups. She was not responding, but woke up when the ambulance was taking her out of our gymnasium, so we all thought she would be alright. She had died within 24 hours of her collapse due to an aneurism that had burst in her brain. So all my teammates were very concerned about me...fearful that I could possibly suffer the same fate. But when I walked into practice after getting out of the hospital, there was a feeling of unity that I hadn't felt before. It's been said that tragedy brings people closer together. In this case, I have to admit that's an accurate statement.

I told Mom many years later about how I tricked her into not making me go to church, and how God taught me a lesson about lying to get out of something he specifically told me to do. You see, God told me to go to church that morning...several times, and I still was the disobedient, rebellious child to him as I was to my mother.  He spoke loudly and clearly to me that day and firmly

reminded me that I can't beat him at anything.  Mom just smiled and

nodded...she didn't need to say one word.  God had already said it for her!

## Chapter 7 – The Change in Tide

A couple of years went by with much of the same thing happening. Junior and I did our best to try to keep our sanity and hold it together, but then, I started to notice a change. Favoritism started to come into play. I was Dad's favorite, and Junior was Mom's favorite...or so it seemed. I didn't understand it. It seemed like Junior could do no wrong, then Dad would come to my defense and take up for me. There were times when Dad would be brutally rude to Junior and Mom would come to his defense. Junior would want to respond, but Mom would not let him. I guess she wanted to protect him, but she did not understand the harm that she was causing. I remember the one time that Dad had said something to Junior that had upset him so bad that he went into the bathroom and locked himself in. I called his name and tried to talk to him, but couldn't get an answer. Luckily, the plastic knob on the door was broken, so I could get a simple butter knife, stick it through the hole in the knob, and push the lock on the inside to open it. As I opened the door, I found him sitting in the bathroom, rocking back and forth, crying. I tried to talk him, but as I did, his lips were moving, but there was no sound coming from his mouth. I immediately ran to Mom and told her and she entered the bathroom and talked to Junior. At this point, I think Dad realized that he had crossed a line he shouldn't have and apologized to Junior. That was a first, but a welcomed one!

The battles continued between Mom and Dad. There was the fight in which Dad hit mom and broke her nose. It was bleeding pretty badly, but all he kept saying was "Shut up and don't say another word." She kept blowing her nose, even though I advised her not to. We finally talked Dad into taking her to the hospital, and it was confirmed that her nose was broken, and because she kept blowing her nose, it could not be properly reset. It caused a slight deformity in the appearance of her nose.

Then there was the fight that arose where Mom had a nervous breakdown. Dad was verbally cutting her down so badly that she began to cry heavily and couldn't breathe. She started to shake uncontrollably and I had never seen her in this condition before. I didn't know what to do. She proceeded to go into the bathroom, climbed into the bathtub, and just sat there crying...rocking back and forth saying, "Oh God...Jesus please help!" Dad refused to take her to the hospital, so I called the ambulance to come and get her. Once again, we finally talked Dad into going to the hospital to get Mom and bringing her back home. There was peace for the rest of that night.

One day, I had enough of the fighting. Dad was threatening to hurt mom once again. I was 17 at the time. I walked into the kitchen where Dad was standing over Mom who was sitting in her usual chair in the kitchen. I said to him, "Move away from her and leave her alone." He rudely stated, "You're a child and you need to remember your place and stay in it." I told him again, "Get away from her and leave her alone or else I will make you." He spun around and said, "Oh, now that you're 17 you think you're big enough to take me? Do it then!" He shouldn't have said that. Mom was telling me to stop, but I wasn't listening. Dad swung at me and missed, and I shoved him into the barbecue grill that we kept in the kitchen when it wasn't in use. He cut his hand when he fell against it, and once he saw the blood, he was out to kill me...literally. I ran into the bedroom with Dad in hot pursuit, cursing and swearing he was going to take my life. I immediately shut the door, sat on the floor and placed my back against my brother's bed that was located closer to the door. I extended my legs with my feet against the door to keep him from entering, but Dad was so angry, that as he pressed against the door to try to get to me, Junior's bed was actually moving. I screamed at Junior, "Help me keep Dad out," but he just sat there looking at me shaking his head no. I think he was pretty scared. Dad kept screaming, "Open the door," and I kept screaming, "No." I guess I was more determined, so Dad finally gave up and went away. Yes, the taste of victory.

Our bedroom was at the west end of the trailer with a window facing south and a window facing west. We lived right off of Highway 50, so anytime an ambulance or sheriff car was rushing to a call, Dad would come into the bedroom and look out the west window, which was directly over my bed, to see where they were going. He would watch them until they were out of site, then proceed with whatever he was previously doing. For many years, I would be in a deep sleep, then suddenly awaken with the feeling that someone was watching me in the middle of the night. Dad would be standing by the side of my bed when I woke up, and when I asked what he was doing, he would say, "I'm looking at the sheriff going down the road…go back to sleep." But, I also noticed that I would have strange dreams, and in my dreams, I would feel very strange sensations. It was during some of those dreams that I would awaken and find him standing next to my bed looking out the window. Many years later I figured out what those strange feelings were, and one particular event that happened helped me to put all the pieces of the puzzle together a few years ago.

My junior year in high school, I would ride my bike to school and back home on nice days. I was on the track team, so this was extra exercise for me and only helped my cause. One day I was home alone with Dad. I can't remember where Junior was. But, I was sitting in a chair watching TV when Dad walked up behind me, put his hands on my shoulders, and began to proposition me. He began to ask me if I knew how to do certain things. (Of course not. After all, I have not had one single date, held hands, kissed, or let a boy put their arms around me. How am I supposed to know about these things?) I answered "no" to every question he asked and felt more and more uncomfortable with each question. He finally said, "Keep this between you and me and don't tell anyone else." Once again, wrong thing to say to me. The next day, I rode my bike to school, but instead of coming home, I rode to Mom's office. She was shocked to see me and asked what I was doing there. I immediately started crying and could hardly get the words out, but I finally forced them out. Mom was not a happy woman, and there's nothing more dangerous than an angry black woman!

The next argument that happened turned the tide in her favor. Dad did not know it, but Mom was watching him one day when he was looking for something in the dresser and saw where he hid his pistol. When he was not home, she grabbed it and hid it somewhere else. Dad started his usual drunken arguing with

Mom, and when he got tired of talking to her without her responding, he went to bed. Mom went and pulled the pistol, cocked it, woke him up, and placed it to his head. She proceeded to speak to him and say, "I know all about what you did to Brenda. If you ever touch Junior or Brenda, or even lifted a hand against them again, I will kill you." I think that shocked and scared Dad into a submission he thought he'd always hold over Mom. Mom outsmarted Dad and gained her freedom. But the true freedom came when he passed away in 1987 from heart failure. He always swore that Mom placed a curse on him because of extreme pain he felt once when she touched him to wake him up. It wasn't a curse, but the force of the tide changing. The rip tide was pulling him out into the deep and he could no longer fight it, but Mom was standing peacefully, watching the waves break and letting them flow over her. She was enjoying the freedom of allowing the waves to flow gently over her feet…knowing that she was safe and out of danger. I was married to my first husband when Dad passed away, and felt the changing tide as well, not realizing the rip tide I was about to get caught in myself.

## Chapter 8 – The Rip Tide

I had left home at the age 18 to attend bible college in Kansas City, MO. This was the fall of 1982, right after I graduated from high school. The trip had already been made to view the campus, and I was excited to get away from home. The day I left for Kansas City was a sad one for me. Dad was still living then, but I was leaving Mom and Junior alone with him, and somehow, I felt I was leaving them unprotected. As I climbed aboard the Amtrak train headed for Kansas City, I had mixed feelings about leaving home, but I knew at some point, it was bound to happen. I sat down in my seat next to the window, and as I looked out, there stood Mom and Junior looking back at me. Junior and I had our differences. We fought with each other most of our lives as many siblings do, but this day, he was actually crying because I was leaving. It broke my heart to see him cry and I wanted to just get up and walk off the train so he would stop, but ' destiny was calling.

I arrived at the college, began the registration process, and got settled into the dorm. The dorm was actually a house that was a few blocks away from the college. There were about 4 other girls who lived there besides me and the dorm mother. After being there for a few months, I began to realize how much I did not like it. Everyone was so strict. We could not wear pants at all...at the college or at the dorm, and they even tried to say that I couldn't wear them when I went to visit family off campus. So, any jeans, sweatpants, or slacks that I had brought with me were immediately disposed of. My grades were pretty good, but I could not handle the legality of the religious rules created by the leadership of the school. After a couple of months, I secured a part-time job at the University of Kansas Medical Center in Kansas City, KS. I worked in a physiology lab and helped to take care of the lab animals and process the results of tests that my boss was performing. This was the first job I really obtained on my own, so it was very important to me. I went home for Christmas and decided that I would not return to school, but I wanted to keep my job. My boss and I discussed it, and he decided to keep me on as a full time assistant. Mom had plenty of family in Kansas City, so arrangements were made for me to stay with an older relative in Kansas City, KS. I was making $4.25 per hour, which in 1983 was a pretty good salary. I paid my cousin to stay in her home out of each paycheck I received, but I soon found out that I had to buy my own food as well, and things started to turn chaotic. I had also been saving money in an account that I started once I became full time, so I decided it was time to move out and live on my own. I found a one-bedroom apartment right off the plaza area of Kansas City, MO which is a very nice neighborhood, and moved in. The location was perfect seeing that my job was just a 10 minute walk away, shopping was about a 10 minute walk away (although it was very expensive), and the grocery story was right around the corner from me. I soon was able to purchase furniture and everything I needed to feel at home. Now, I was set.

Dad also had family that lived in Kansas City, MO, and I decided to spend the 4th of July with them. His sister and family lived across town, but I was so used to taking the public transit everywhere that it was not a problem to get there at all. While I was visiting, I met a young man who lived across the street from them. He was the same age as me and we began to talk. The next thing I knew, we had started dating. This was a scary thing for me as Dad had been so very protective of me. I never dated in high school, never went to a dance, and never had the opportunity to even have a decent conversation with anyone of the opposite sex. Everyone was so afraid of him that they avoided me. Now, I had someone showing me attention, and I was soaking it up deeply. He had a lot of things going on and couldn't spend a whole lot of time with me, so we began to grow apart, but we still kept in contact with each other.

My Aunt was a member of the Seventh Day Adventist Church and invited me to go with her. Church was a big part of my life and something that I determined would continue to be so until I left this world. Being without church to me was like a fish being without water, and I was searching for one that would meet my needs and provide the spiritual food that I was hungry for. While at church, a man was visiting and came up to sing a special. He was tall, slender, and handsome looking. The pianist did not know the song he was singing, but I did. There were advantages to having a mom that was an entertainer. She had taught me how to read music and how to play piano by ear. So, after church was over, I approached him and offered to play for him the next time he visited the church. We struck up a conversation about music and somehow a dinner date was accomplished.

A couple of days later, he stopped by as promised, and we went out to dinner. We walked around the plaza for a bit then came back to my place. I knew how the public transit ran and knew the last bus to Kansas City, KS would soon be running and advised him that he should be on his way. Of course there was more he wanted to talk about and the goodbye kiss he wanted to give me turned into much more. He forced himself on me sexually and it was then that I realized what those strange sensations were that I felt as a child. I screamed at him, "Get off of me" because I did not like what I was feeling, but he very adamantly said, "I'm not through yet. I'll get off of you when I'm finished." It really wasn't what he said that scared me, it was the look on his face. By the time he had finished, he had missed the last bus, and was telling me about how this elderly lady was allowing him to stay in her home, and how he was helping to take care of her. With it being so late, she would not let him into the house, so he pleaded with me to let him stay with me for the night. This man was in church, and even though something happened that I didn't like, it was a one-time thing and it wouldn't happen again, right? It was decided that he could sleep on the couch, but he had to leave first thing in the morning...and he did.

Later that evening, he came back with bags of clothes saying, "The woman I'm staying with has thrown me out and I have nowhere to go." I, like my mom was very compassionate and kind hearted, and did not like seeing anyone hurting or struggling. So I let him move in. I had been sucked into the rip tide. I saw it, recognized it, but still swam right into it. Mom had always said, "I don't care who you marry as long as they love you, take care of you, and do nothing to hurt you. If those conditions are met, I will be happy with whomever you marry." She also prayed that I wouldn't find and marry someone like Dad...that prayer was short lived. Soon, the true personality of this person I was trying to help started to show.  I would not do what he commanded me to do, so he hit me.  I was determined to not be in the same boat as mom, so I gave him a very hard right hook to the left side of his face which stunned him.  I angrily yelled, "You are not to lay your hands on me again, or you will suffer the consequences."  That action dazed him for a little while, but I soon found myself drowning in the rip tide, taking in water, and not being able to breathe.  I couldn't tell mom, even though she had the means to pull me out.  I just couldn't bring myself to tell her I had gotten myself involved with a man just like Dad and break her heart.  This was something I had to do on my own.  Her side of the family was very serious about protecting their own, and one of her brothers had actually done time for killing someone, so this was something that had to be kept a secret and handled by me alone.  At least I thought I could handle it alone.

## Chapter 9 – Attempted Rescues

The next few months would prove to be very trying. Since I now had this new person living with me, things were turning for the worst very quickly. I had a neighbor below me who had a little girl that I babysat pretty frequently. We talked all the time, and we decided to swap information for emergency purposes. I had her phone information and she had mine. She had my mom's phone number, my aunt's phone number, and my work phone number. She was pretty concerned about this new person I had allowed into my life, but she wasn't the only one. My aunt had this very annoying habit of running checks on people. She was a librarian and always had the connections to find out about anybody. Once she found out about the living situation, she called me and proceeded to ask if I knew that this person had 4 children back in Little Rock, Arkansas and 1 in Kansas City, KS. Of course he had told me everything, so that did not concern me.

He had tried to force himself on me again at one point and I struggled to fight back. I soon found out that I wasn't as physically strong as I thought I was. Déjà vu happened as he slapped me across the face and left his hand print on the left side of my face. As Mom often did, I covered it with makeup and came up with the appropriate story, "I was curling my hair and the curling iron slipped."

My neighbor had seen the injury and asked what happened. Of course I told her the story and tried to make it as believable as possible, but I could see that she was not believing me. Without me knowing it, she had called my aunt, who began trying to contact me. I did not want family involved with this and already felt embarrassed about it, so I avoided family at all costs. I continued to take care of the injury the best I could to get it to heal quicker and it was working. Thank God it healed because a few days later there was a knock at my door. Mom had come in from Colorado and my aunt came over with her to check on me since they could not get hold of me. I refused to open the door for a few moments, but then I couldn't resist the voice of Mom any longer. As I opened the door, she asked, "How are you doing?" Then she bluntly asked, "Has someone been beating up on you?" I had done such a great job of taking care of the injury that it had completely healed and there was not even a scar to substantiate any type of abuse. So, I lied and said, "Nothing has happened to me, Mom. I'm fine." Mom felt uneasy about leaving, but there was no proof that anything was going on, so she went back home. Mom had thrown me a lifeline and I refused to take it.

The following weeks and months proved to be disastrous. I lost my job at KU Medical Center, and was about to lose my apartment. I found another job working for McDonald's, but suffered a workman's compensation injury and had to leave it as well.  This meant my so-called roommate would have to leave the comfort of the nest and find employment himself.  He soon found work, but his concern was not me or the apartment.  He would come in drunk or smelling of marijuana.  And to make matters worse, this 30 plus year old man began hanging out with teenagers…yes, teenagers!  He brought them into the apartment and threatened to hurt me if I said anything about it.  I actually complained and was punched in the face in front of these kids.  He brought the dope into the apartment, and had the kids smoking it.  If I remember correctly, there were two girls and two boys.  I found out that one of the girls was a runaway and the police were looking for her.  It was then that I realized I had a legal reason for putting them out of the apartment, and he had no choice but to submit to my command.  They left the apartment, but decided to hang out in the basement storage area of the building I resided in.  They were caught and the young girl returned to her parents.

The manager of the complex called and wanted to talk to me the next day.  She understood my job situation, and spoke with the owners. They were willing to work with me to help me keep the apartment because I had been such a model resident, but there was one stipulation…he had to leave.  Once again that kindhearted side took over.  Why couldn't I let go of this person?  I was about to lose everything and I was choosing him.  He sarcastically told me, "Go back home

to your momma where you belong. You can't make it anyway."  That really hurt

and just encouraged me more to stay.  The manager had thrown me another

lifeline, and like my Mom's, I refused to grab it and allow someone to pull me to

safety.  I wasn't about to admit failure to anyone, and I had nowhere to go and no

place to keep my belongings.  So I turned my keys into the office, and we walked

the streets by day while he tried to find work, and at night, we would sneak back

into my storage unit in the basement of the building I used to live in.  There, we

slept on the hard floor.  It was cold, but at least we weren't out in the elements in

the middle of March while there was snow on the ground.  But, we were

discovered and banished from ever setting foot on the property again.  So now, I

was truly homeless.  This man that was supposed to be so interested in me had

caused me to lose everything I had, including my self-esteem.  I was now destined

to wander the streets like a vagabond, and I knew I was so much better than this.

Every now and then, we would come across a church that was having service, and

would attend.  Most times, they were looking for a musician, and he made it

known that I could play piano.  I felt like I was "prostituting" my gift, but this

would give us food to eat and a temporary roof over our head for a few days.  The

only problem is, when it was all said and done, the pastors were interested in me and not him.  This would upset him, and I once again would be forced out into the streets...not knowing where my next meal or source of heat was coming from. This was another lifeline thrown that I refused to grab.  Why couldn't I allow myself to swim out of this rip tide?  I was purposely placing myself in it, and I knew better.  I had several opportunities for rescue, but was refusing them.  What was wrong with me?

One day, in a grocery store, we met a lady in the checkout line.  We began talking, and she invited us to a church where, as she put it, "You can experience the move of God."  They were having a revival at the time with an evangelist from California.  So she gave us the name of the church and the address.  That night, we made it a point to be there.  It was very powerful and the evangelist was quite dynamic.  As the evangelist opened the altar call, he said, "There's someone here struggling to find their way."  My so-called companion started making his way to the altar, and once again urged me to go back home to mamma and quit following him, but like a little puppy, I followed him to the altar.  He explained our situation to the evangelist, and by the end of the evening, one of the church mothers had opened up her home to us.  Not only that, but the evangelist was offering to help us to obtain all the paperwork to get married.  I sincerely believed I was in love with this person, but more than that, I didn't want to have to claim that I was unable to make it on my own. So without any pre-marital counseling, one week later, we were married during one of the revival services. My head was above water now, and I could breathe. I could see the horizon and knew where I was now. I finally reached out and grabbed a lifeline, and felt I was finally being pulled to safety, but was there actually someone at the other end of the lifeline, or was I floating aimlessly? I wasn't sure, but at least my wandering days were over, and that meant the world to me.

## Chapter 10 – Dry Land

I was out of the rip tide, and I could see dry land now.  I was ready to step onto solid ground, get my footing, and run with all my might.  I was so ready for this….but discovered I was not headed for land, I was drifting away from it.  How could this be?  I was doing all the right things…I had started going to church, and I was no longer living in sin…I was married.  However, in the midst of me doing all the right things, my husband was now verbally abusing me under the roof of the church mother, who reported it to the pastor.  Several meetings for marital counseling were set up and attended, but very few of them did any good.  Feeling that we were being spied upon and that our privacy was being violated, he decided that it was time to leave her house, and move out into our own.  I agreed…maybe this would put him in a better mood and he wouldn't be so awful to people, especially me.  How wrong I was!

We found a cheap little apartment in Kansas City, Kansas that was affordable.  I had found employment with a microfilming company and he with a grocery store.  We continued to attend church, and he eventually received his minister's license and was one of the many associate pastors that the senior pastor was training.  But, soon his old ways returned.  One minute he was the godly minister, the next he was the abuser.  He went back and forth so much, that I didn't know which one to expect at any given time.

Our apartment did not have the usual deadbolt locks on the doors, so we had to padlock them anytime we left.  When he was not in his "minister" mode, it wasn't unusual for him to go out, drink and party all night long and never come back home.  The only problem is...he would padlock me in the apartment...and we were on the 2$^{nd}$ floor.  Can you imagine what it would be like to call your employer the next day and say, "I can't make it into work today because my husband padlocked me in the apartment?"  Most times, I don't think they believed me, but when I started showing up to work with bruises, black eyes, and contusions on my face, it made them believers.  It was not unusual for him to sleep with other women, even women in the very church we attended.  I would find out about them and threaten bodily harm, but, there was always someone to step in and diffuse the situation.  Needless to say, the minister's license was finally taken away from him.

Most times, I would cash my check and bring it home only to have him attack me, pin me down, go through my pockets or purse, and take every last penny I had.  At times, we had no money for food or anything else.  There were times I lived off of Cherry Chan and Lemonhead candy because that's all I had money for after he stole all the rest of it. He would spend it on booze, dope, women, and his drinking buddies doing God knows what. I finally had to get wise and get money orders for rent, so at least it was paid.

The worst beating came at a time when he very nonchalantly told me, "I don't love you and I don't want you anymore." He wanted me out of the apartment (though I was the one paying for it), and didn't want to see me again. But, he padlocked me in, so I couldn't go anywhere. He was gone all day long, so I was left in the apartment to try and figure out how to get him to change his mind about me. When he came back, he was not alone. He had an ex-girlfriend with him, and immediately said, "I want you to go into the bedroom and stay there." Of course I was to do this while he and she sat in the living room. I stayed for a minute, then came out and said, "I need to talk to you." He hollered back, "Get back into the bedroom and stay there!" Once again I sat down on the bed, and the anger began to rise within me. I rose up, opened the door, walked out again and angrily said, "I need to speak to you, and she needs to leave MY apartment!" This time, he screamed at me, using every bit of intimidation he had within him and said, "Get back into the bedroom. I don't love you, and I don't want you. You're worthless. What part of this do you not understand?" He was saying all of this in front of his ex-girlfriend to try to embarrass me into doing what he wanted.

I refused to do what he asked, so he began to beat me...in front of the other

woman, who sat there and did nothing the whole time. I had my clothes ripped

off, my hair pulled, I was drug across the floor, and was kicked in the stomach

numerous times. I was punched, and beaten with a boat oar that was left in the

apartment by a previous tenant. Still, this ex-girlfriend did nothing. I had been

experiencing nausea a few days prior to the event and suspected that I could be

pregnant. When I had expressed this to him earlier, he said, "You can't be

pregnant, and if you are, it more than likely isn't mine." Please! Give me a break!

Unless I was experiencing an immaculate conception, that was impossible. I cried,

"God, please forgive him for taking the life of my unborn child" as he was kicking

me repeatedly in my stomach. I hadn't had the pregnancy confirmed yet, but I

just knew that I was, and I was pleading with God to spare his or her life. After

the beating, he said, "Go to bed. I want you out of here the first thing tomorrow

morning." I was in too much pain to argue with him, so I went to bed. A few

minutes later, he came into the bedroom with his ex-girlfriend, so all three of us

were lying in the bed, fully clothed. Every time I would try to leave, he would

reach over and grab me and ask where I was going, then wouldn't let me move.

The next morning, when everyone was awake, he looked at my face and asked, "What happened to you?" How could he not remember beating me the night before? I'm surprised he didn't have sore muscles from the beating he administered the night before. I looked him squarely in the face and said, "You did this to me! Do you not remember what you did?" With a surprised look on his face, he simply stated, "I can't believe I did all that to you! I'm so sorry!" The ex-girlfriend confirmed everything, but it didn't change his demeanor. He decided to get up and walk her home that morning. After he left, I rose up to go to the bathroom and felt the worst pain I had ever felt in my lower stomach and back, and I started to bleed profusely. I managed to call for a cab and asked them to take me to a hospital. Due to the nature of the trip, the driver did not charge me a penny, which I was very thankful for. As I went into the emergency room, I prayed, "God, please spare the life of my child if I'm indeed pregnant." My instincts proved to be correct. I had been pregnant...three months pregnant to be exact, and the beating had caused a miscarriage. My heart was crushed to no end, and the pain from it was unimaginably worse than the physical pain I was feeling. I cried for days, but couldn't tell him why. I felt he didn't deserve to know. He took something special away from me, and nothing would ever change that fact. Many more things happened in the following months, but it took me 20 years to forgive him for taking away from me the most precious thing in the

world.  But I soon realized that this was the first blessing in disguise.  God knew

what was best for me, and I had to believe and trust that he did.

## Chapter 11 – The Road to Freedom

Times continued to be very difficult for me. I was still plagued by the money problems caused by my husband's careless squandering, and it was taking its toll. I worked in downtown Kansas City, MO but lived in Kansas City, KS, which meant I had to get up every morning and catch a bus to take me across the state line. At times when I didn't have the bus fare, I would borrow from people at work and pay them back when I got paid. When I couldn't borrow money, that meant I had to walk to work, which was about a two mile walk. Two miles doesn't seem like a long way, but walking those two miles at 6:00 in the morning, when it's still dark outside, walking through unlit, unsafe, deserted industrial areas, it's a scary walk. Many a morning, I knew there were angels walking with me because I was never attacked or approached by anyone. It was especially difficult when the weather was less than favorable, but my husband did not care...about my health, about my safety, about me. But yet, I still loved him, and wanted him to love me more than anything else. We fought and argued, and I found creative ways to make him pay attention to me, except it caused negative attention. I would write letters to a make-believe love interest and leave them lying around for him to find...not right out in the open, but in places where he wouldn't have to look hard for them. At one point, I think he actually took them to our pastor, and the pastor decided to have another counseling session. Did this mean that he actually still had feelings for me and was jealous of this make-believe person, or was he playing a game of tattle tell to make me look like the enemy? The latter was the case, but once pastor talked to me and found out why I did it, the plan backfired. The verbal abuse was worse.

In a drunken stupor he had wandered back home one morning and started screaming at me for no apparent reason. I, like my mom, had figured out that when I said nothing, it made him angrier because I wouldn't fuel the fire, and he would eventually leave the apartment. But this time, when he left, he made a promise...he said, "I'm going to buy a gun and when I get back, I will show you who is in control." This really did scare me, and seeing that Mom had gone through this as well, I gave her a call. Surprisingly, she was very calm about it. "Hang up the phone and call the police," she said. "Then call your auntie to come and pick you up." I did just that. We had gotten into a physical confrontation the night before, so some of the bruising was still visible. A couple of police officers showed up about 10 minutes after I called and began to talk to me. I began to tell them about the abuse, about him locking me in the apartment, and finally about him going to get a gun. One of the officers took a look at my face and immediately noticed the injury. He asked, "Do you have a safe place to go?" I answered, "Yes, my aunt is on her way to pick me up." As I began to pack up

some things to take with me, both officers were beginning to look around the

apartment when my husband showed up. By this time, three officers were at my

apartment. I immediately backed up behind one of the officers who noticed the

fear on my face. He turned and asked me, "Do you want to press charges?" I was

scared and didn't know what to say in the presence of my husband who was

cursing loudly and calling me names in the background. The officer stood in front

of me to block me from the view of my husband and said, "Nothing is going to

happen to you, that's why we're here. Do you want to press charges?" Through

my tears, I was able to mumble a faint "yes." My husband walked right passed

them into the kitchen and opened the freezer. Not knowing whether he had a

gun or not, they turned, pulled out their weapons and hollered, "Sir, please come

out of the kitchen, with your hands up!" He immediately answered, "I'm getting

something out of the freezer for my neighbor next door." The officers hollered

once again, "Sir, please come out now, with your hands in the air." He hollered

back, "I heard you, let me get a beer out of the freezer for my friend next door!"

This time, the tone changed in the officers' voices, and I feared that I was going to

see someone get shot or killed that day. The third time, they said, "Come out

now with your hands up or we will shoot!" They repeated this a few times, and he finally obeyed their orders. The one officer who had spoken to me earlier saw how distraught I was and decided to take me out and place me in his car. He began to take my statement, and as I shakily began to answer his questions, he was very calming and patient with me. I looked up and saw my handcuffed husband being placed into the back of another police car to be taken to jail. The officer assured me that I would be safe and proceeded to complete the statement. This officer was about my age, 22 or 23 years of age. He was about 6 feet in height, with blond hair and blue eyes, and had very muscular build. I couldn't help but to be infatuated by this gorgeous "knight in shining armor" who had come and rescued me from the "evil villain" that day. He gave me his business card with all the phone numbers on it and said, "You will need to appear in court on this date. You will most likely want to file for a restraining order to protect yourself from further harm. I will be there in the courtroom on this date to support you, and if you need anything at all, you can contact or reach me at any of the numbers listed on the card." Wow, could there really be someone that cared this much? And, if so, why didn't I end up with him? This officer seemed to have genuine concern for me, I knew it was his job to care. But, can't a girl dream a little?

As I sat in the back of my aunt's car, I watched the police car drive away with my husband in the back seat. I knew that I was now safe, but I couldn't help but to feel a little sorry for the guy. After all, this is the man I fell in love with and married, right? As the tears rolled down my face, comforting words came from my aunt, "It will be alright," she said. "You're safe now, and you can stay with us as long as you want until you get back on your feet." We arrived at her home 30 minutes later, and a feeling came over me like none other I had ever felt. I was happy to be out of the abuse, but my heart had been crushed into a million different pieces. The man I loved was in jail, and now at 22 years of age, I had been forced to live with family...a move I had been very successful in avoiding up to this point. Maybe it was just embarrassment, but I sure felt like my world had come to an end. I made her promise not to tell the rest of the family due to the violent nature of some of them. I did want my husband to pay for what he did, but I did have a heart and didn't want him dead. She made sure I made it to the bus stop to catch my buses to get to work on time, and was there to pick me up when the bus dropped me off in the evenings. I stayed with her and my uncle for the whole month leading up to the court date for the assault, and it was peaceful and quiet. For once I had found my road for freedom, and was on my way to bigger and brighter things.

The court date finally arrived, and my aunt dropped me off at the courthouse. I had a whole month to decide what I wanted to do and how to proceed...I would continue to stay with my aunt for a while, and request that my husband get anger management counseling through our pastor. If that went well, then, we would talk about possible reconciliation. As I walked into the court room, there sat my husband...looking so sad and sullen, like he had lost every friend he had in the world. As he looked up and saw me, he smiled and waved. I immediately gave a quick wave and tried to avoid eye contact him. Patiently waiting for our case to come before the judge, I kept going over what I was going to say to the judge in my head, "Ok, I would like to request anger management for my husband for a period of no less than 90 days, and yes, I would like to continue forward with the charges!" I was abruptly brought back to reality by the sound of my name being called. As I walked to stand before the judge, my legs felt as if they were going to fall out from beneath me at any time. "Breathe," I thought to myself as I positioned myself in front of the desk of the judge. "How do you plead?" the judge asked my husband. "Not guilty," he snuggly replied. "NOT GUILTY?" How could he plead not guilty when there was ample evidence against him everywhere? There was a blur of rapidly thrown questions that seemed to whiz by my head, then it was my turn. "Do you want to move forward with the charges, and do you want me to issue a restraint order?" the judge asked. My head was hollering out "YES, YES, YES," but what came out of my mouth shocked me. "If he decides to take anger management counseling from our pastor for 3 months, I'll drop the charges." What just came out of my mouth? I couldn't believe I had just said that. The judge confirmed with me what my decision was and stated that the case could be reopened again within the following 60 days if anything happened. As I walked out of the courtroom, I just wanted to run; somewhere...anywhere. How could I have let this man off the hook again after what he had put me through? What is wrong with me? I knew I had to catch a bus to get back out to my Aunt's house, so I walked as fast as I could to get away from him, but he ran up, placed his arms around me, and gave me the biggest hug and kiss...in public. This man never showed public affection, but now he's decided to start. "Let me go...I've got to catch a bus and go home," I said as I tried to fight off the tears welling up inside of me. "You need to come back to your real home," he stated. "I've missed you so much, and I'm sorry about what I've done to you. I've scheduled counseling appointments with pastor and will begin them next week, so I hope you will support me." After a few moments of bantering back and forth, I gave in and walked back to the apartment with him. It seemed like old times again, when I was the only woman he wanted. He showed me the attention I was longing for in the relationship, and as it was getting late, I decided to stay the night with him and go back to my aunt's the next day.  Finally, things were beginning to fall back into place, and I had my husband back, or so I thought. I moved back into the apartment with him, and my family was not happy about it, but it was my life, and my choice.  I was going to make this relationship work through hell or high water.  I was not going to fail at this.

## Chapter 12 – The Big Move

After a while of living at the deteriorating apartment, we decided it was time for us to make a move. We had searched and found some nice little townhomes on the northeast side of Kansas City. The price was right, and the places were decent. So, we leased a one bedroom townhome with our own basement which included a washer and dryer. We were both working at the time, so we were able to purchase new furniture and other things for the apartment. Just when I thought things were on the upswing, it began to happen again...the checking my purse for phone numbers, checking my underwear drawers for signs of God knows what. He was at it again...accusing me of cheating on him. We had just moved into the new apartments, and I didn't know anyone...who was I going to cheat on him with? It began to get worse and worse, but I didn't know how bad it was going to get.

After being there for a few months, he began leaving for work in the mornings (or so he said) and not coming home until very early the next morning...usually around 1:00 or 2:00 am. Sometimes he didn't come home at all. I had a dream one night that a lot of women were surrounding him, and I became very angry and began to cry. In the dream he looked at me, smiled and said,

"Don't worry...there's enough of me to go around." That was a warning sign for me, but I wasn't prepared for what followed approximately a month after the dream.

He had begun to tell me that he didn't love me anymore, and that there was someone else he had fallen in love with. "He's just trying to be mean and hurt me as usual," I kept telling myself. It was our 2 year anniversary, and I had decided to make a nice candlelight dinner for the both of us to enjoy...soft music in the background...incense burning...awwww if this didn't change his attitude or feelings towards me, I didn't know what would. Well, it didn't. He was supposed to be home by 5:00. At 6:00 he still was not home. 7:30...still not home. 10:00...still not home. I finally went to bed at 1:00 am...he still was not home. That night was a very sleepless night for me. "Was he alright? Who was he with and what was he doing? Out of all the nights of the year, why would he choose to do this to me on our anniversary?" These thoughts kept running through my head all night long, and I couldn't decide whether to be scared, concerned, or angry.

I was getting ready to go to the church on Saturday morning to a function they were having. As I was walking out the door of the apartment, something told me to check in the basement. My husband had been known to lock himself

in there for hours at a time watching a little portable television that we had

placed there to make our laundry days a little less tedious. I walked down the

stairs, unlocked the door, and in the dark, noticed that some of our clothes that

we had stored in the basement were on the floor. I turned on the light and

noticed they were scattered on the floor with a blanket on top. But wait...there

was one person under the blanket, which was him, and...there's another person

there too. As I yanked the blanket back, I discovered him lying on the floor along

with a girl (who was younger than me by the way) undressed from the waist

down. I spoke out his name and the girl opened her eyes and saw me...what

looked back at me was fear. I called his name out again, and he rolled over and

placed his arm around her body, the way he used to hold me. At that point, every

bit of anger in my body took over and I gained strength from a place I never

realized existed. I grabbed the girl's shirt and lifted her off the floor, holding her

several feet in the air. I slammed her against the wall and began to beat her. The

words I spoke at that time were not the words to be spoken by a godly woman,

nevertheless, they got his attention. He immediately jumped up and stepped in

between me and her and caught one of my blows intended for her. His

response...he punched me back. But, for some reason, that punch did not phase me. I lunged back to get past him to her and he hollered, "Stop, Brenda...leave her alone. I told you I didn't love you anymore, just go back upstairs." This fueled my anger more, and as I continued my assault on the unidentified girl, he placed himself between me and her again...this time with his back facing me. As I stormed back up the stairs, my neighbor's boyfriend was heading out to work and asked, "Is everything ok? Are you alright?" Between the tears of hurt and anger, all I could muster out was, "No, I'm not ok." I can't remember who he said he worked for, but he gave me his business card with information on it and said if I needed anything, he would be able to get me assistance. I am so thankful for him stopping me that day, because if he hadn't been there at that time, I may have been writing this book from a prison cell somewhere in Missouri. God always knows who to place in your path at any given moment.

As I left the apartment, I ran, full stride, all the way to the bus stop which was about half a mile away. I just wanted to get away from all the drama and find someplace I could think and get some help. I hopped on the bus and ended up at my church about 1 hour later. After arriving at the church, I noticed I had hurt my hand in the fight and it was bleeding...not badly, but enough to catch my attention. As I walked into the administrative office, the secretary saw my face and asked, "What's wrong?" I immediately began weeping uncontrollably as if my very being was going to jump out of my body. I tried to tell her what happened, but I was weeping so hard that I couldn't speak. She said, "Let me go get the Bishop, I'll be right back." As I sat in the office, I could only imagine what he would say. We had been counseling with him in regards to our marriage issue for some time, now it had taken another turn for worse. As he walked in, he took one look at me and said, "Daughter, what happened?" Immediately the weeping started again...years of anger, pain, hurt, frustration, and depression had now come to a head, and the lid of the pressure cooker had fully blown off. Finally, I calmed down enough to tell him what happened, which upset him a bit. The secretary noticed my injury, and was able to dress it, as it was small. Bishop asked, "Have you called the police and made a report?" "No, not yet," I answered. He then instructed the secretary to contact a domestic violence shelter and find out what needed to be done. They confirmed that I needed to go to a police station and that an officer would take me to the shelter. As God would have it, the police station was only a few blocks away, so I walked there. I entered into the station, told them about the situation, and within 10 minutes was sitting in the front a police car being transported to the shelter. Once again, a police officer was saving my life.

I was escorted into the shelter, and I remember, for the first time since the incident, I felt fear. I walked into this shelter with nothing but the clothes on my back, my purse, my bible, and whatever money I had in my possession. I didn't know what to expect, let alone know what a battered women's shelter was. But, the people there treated me with kindness and respect. Once I was processed in, I was given the tour of the place. At the time, work was being done on the shelter. There were 4 floors, and only the first floor was ready for residents. After the tour, I was taken to their basement where I could go through donated clothing to pick out some things to wear and was given a bag containing soap, toothpaste shampoo, etc. There were 2 girls per room and each room had 2 double beds in them. Not quite the Hilton, but enough to bring peace of mind and comfort. I was told not to disclose the address or location of the shelter because of safety reasons. Under no circumstance was I to relay any of this information to anyone.

The first night was very rough. I cried most of the night, and was up part of it talking with one of the counselors there. It just seemed like I couldn't get that ole faucet to shut off. No matter what valves I turned, it just kept running...and running...and running. Finally, I was just too exhausted from the events of the day and all the crying and fell asleep. I was safe; nobody was going to hurt me again.

No more hollering and screaming, no more name calling, and most of all, no more beatings.  It was in January, so the weather was rather chilly, but the next few months would prove to be even colder than the weather.  By the way...that domestic violence shelter that I resided in at that time was...Rose Brooks (in its beginning stages) in Kansas City, MO.  They have grown tremendously since then and have helped so many women to break the cycle of domestic violence.  Had it not been for them, I don't know what I would have done.  So, from the bottom of my heart, Thank You Rose Brooks for all that you do and for all that you've done.  You started me on my way, and look at me now!

## Chapter 13 – Taking a Step Backwards

Life was rather difficult at the shelter. I could not figure out why I loved this man so much, but surely I must be crazy. I had secured a new job with better pay and benefits with a hospital in the area as a patient representative. I was able to still go to work while at the shelter, so it gave me a little free money to keep, plus give some to the shelter as well. I loved my new job, and it looked as if I was coming out the situation on a good note. However, one thing just kept pricking my heart. It was almost Valentine's Day, and I missed my husband so much. There just had to be something that I could do to get him back. I figured that if I couldn't get him back with words, I'd buy him back. So I went to a jewelry store and bought him a nice ring. I had to place it on lay-away for a couple of weeks, but I'd have it in time for Valentine's Day. I purchased the ring, and against the shelter's advice delivered it to him personally on that special day. But the response I received wasn't what I expected. He was at work at the time and was not receptive to me at all. He did like the ring, but again stated that he did not love me and did not have feelings for me anymore. "No, I refuse to accept that and I'm going to keep trying to win him back," my heart kept saying. I begged for another chance to prove to him that I was worthy of his love and time. He grudgingly gave in and decided to give it another try, but made no promises.

After about 2 months of staying at the shelter, I could take it no longer…the hollering, crying children that were throwing temper tantrums could not be disciplined due to the violent environment they came from. So parents were allowed to take their unruly children into a room, wrap their arms around them like a strait jacket, and let the children holler, scream, and or cry until they wore themselves out. This was the first time I was introduced to "Time Out." I was used to immediate action being taken, and the children falling into line. I later understood the purpose of this technique. So, I took a step backwards in the process and moved back with my husband, thinking this would be the time that everything would work out and we would live happily ever after. Things were rocky at first, he gave me the "silent treatment" and would not talk to me for days. I didn't complain when he came home very late or not at all, and I tried to give him as much space as I possibly could to allow him to see that I really cared about him and loved him. Finally, after a couple of weeks, he began to speak to me, and I felt we were making progress…until the day it happened again. The anger flared up once more. I had fixed dinner and he had come in late. He quietly sat down at the table, took one bite, and immediately began to complain about the food. "I thought you knew how to cook…apparently you didn't take after your dad," he snidely remarked. "This food tastes like dog poop (using more appropriate phrasing here), and I'm not going to eat it. You had better fix me something else and do it quick. I don't even know why I married you…all you ever do is screw up everything," he hollered. At that, he picked up the plate of food and threw it…plate and all. It missed my head by a few inches and smashed against the kitchen wall. "I'm going back out, and you had better have my dinner ready when I get back…and clean up this mess!" He barked as he walked out the door of the apartment. All I could do was stand there in shock, not knowing what to do first. Suddenly the tears began to flow heavily. "I've managed to screw up again," I said out loud. "I had tried so hard to make things perfect for him, and he still is not happy with me." I quickly picked up the broken pieces of the glass plate that was scattered on the kitchen floor and cleaned up the food. Then I had the task of trying to figure out what to cook for dinner again, but somehow, I had a feeling he was not coming back that night, so I just disrobed, took a nice hot shower and went to bed. I was right…he never returned to the apartment that night.

As the weeks went by, things began to get increasingly worse again. We fought for what seemed like almost every day or night about something, and I was beginning to realize that it was time to give up this fight and continue this journey called "my life" on my own. One Saturday morning, one of the biggest arguments came about. I can't even remember what it was about, but it escalated to a point that I never thought our arguments would reach. He began cursing and swearing at me, and with his fists clutched to his sides, he began walking towards me in the kitchen. I was cornered with nowhere to go, but reached for a large butcher knife which was in the dish drainer to dry. I immediately placed it in front of me and said, "Stop! If you take one more step towards me, I will kill you!" He took another step, and smiled that sheepish grin he always used when he wanted to play "devil's advocate". I drew the knife back and gave one last warning, "I mean it...stop or I will kill you right here where you stand. I'm not playing!" My whole body was shaking, and I felt as if every last ounce of breath had been sucked out of me. Here I stood, ready to kill another human. Was it in me to do this? I knew I had to defend myself, now that I had the knife. For me to drop it at this point would mean certain extensive injuries or even death by his hand. "If you're going to kill me, you better do it now before I get to you," he hollered at the top of his lungs. As he took one more step towards me, I drew back the knife and closed my eyes so that I wouldn't see what I was about to do, then came that still small voice from heaven saying, "Put the weapon down." It was the voice of the Holy Spirit. "You are protected, and it's not worth you spending the rest of your life in jail over, or going through the rest of your life with killing your husband on your conscience. Let God fight this battle, and listen

for his instruction," he said. I began to cry and slowly dropped the knife to the

floor. "See, I knew it. You're weak and can't do anything right. Don't you ever

pull something like that on me again, or I will kill you," my husband said as he

grabbed me by the arms and threw me against the wall. He angrily grabbed his

wallet, mumbled a few choice words, and then slammed the door as he walked

out. I picked myself up from the floor and realized that now was the time that I

had to make my get away. A few weeks earlier, I had contemplated finding

another place to live on my own, and had found an apartment right up the street

from the hospital where I worked. It was very convenient to be so close that I

could walk to work in a matter of 5 minutes. A deposit had already been made on

the apartment, so now, I had a place to run to. "I have to move quickly before he

comes back," I thought to myself. Even though he had been so terrible to me the

past 3 years, I still had a soft spot in my heart for him. As I started to pack as

much as I could to take with me, I began to feel sorry for him, and decided to take

half of everything...half the dishes, half the silverware, half the bedding, half the

towels, etc. All of this took every bit of 15 minutes to pack. I placed everything

into trash bags, including all my clothing, then called a cab to pick me up and take

me to my new apartment. Anxiously, I waited for the cab to arrive, hoping that my husband would not return before I could make my escape. I was feeling much like a prisoner must feel when contemplating a jail break. Soon I heard the horn honk and knew it was the cab. I wrote a short note explaining that I was leaving and never coming back, then grabbed the bags and drug them outside to the cab; looking around to see if I saw my attacker anywhere. As I looked down at my keychain, I knew there was one last thing that had to be done. With tears welling up once again, I placed the key in an envelope and laid it next to the note I had written, turned the lock on the handle of the door and shut it. As I rode in the cab to my new home, I was saddened once again to know that I had failed at my mission of making my marriage work. The tears freely flowed once again, this time, it felt more like they were cleansing something deep within me. The prison door had opened and I had been exonerated. I was no longer a prisoner in my own home. The cab finally arrived at my new apartment, and the driver helped me to unload everything from the car. I made my way to the management office and paid the 1st month's rent that was required of me, then moved everything into the apartment. I had no bed, and no other furniture, but I was content to sleep on the floor for a little while. For the first time in years, I had the most wonderful, peaceful sleep…I was no longer worried about where my husband was or what he was doing, or if he was going to be angry with me about something.

He was now just a vision of my past blowing away in the wind, and I was

beginning a new journey on my own.

## Chapter 14 – I'm Flying, Baby...Flying

The next year was extraordinary. I had begun work with the hospital through a temporary employment service, and the hospital had decided to bring me on-staff permanently. That meant benefits and higher pay. I loved my work and enjoyed coming into work every day. I had begun to save money in the credit union there, and felt like my life was finally becoming what I felt it should be. I had stopped going to the church that I belonged to because my husband was still going there, and was searching for a new church home. That seemed to be a challenge for me in that I was Pentecostal. My church fellowshipped with many other churches in the area of the same denomination, which put me at risk of meeting up with my husband if I joined any of them. So, for a while, I was like a fish out of water.

Everything was going well for me until an incident happened at the hospital...It caught on fire. One evening, while watching the television, a breaking news story interrupted the program, reporting a fire at the hospital. I immediately ran up the street to find numerous fire trucks there. There apparently wasn't very much fire damage, but there was extensive smoke and water damage. The next morning, we spent lots of time cleaning everything that we could, so that we could get back to work. But, that day also brought surprise and fear. A professional restoration company had been brought in to clean and sterilize everything. I sat in an enclosed area at the back of the office, so I could hear conversations, but could not see anyone. As I was performing my everyday tasks, I heard a couple of gentlemen talking as they were approaching the back area. As they entered my area, I looked up and...one of the men was my husband. My heart immediately sunk to my stomach and I wanted to run away – anywhere to get away from him. He was just as surprised to see me and said, "Hi, how are you doing?" "Fine," I said as I focused my attention back on my work. He continued his attempts to converse with me, which ended with me saying, "Look, I have work to do here. Please do whatever it is that has to be done here, and move on your way." He very chalantly said "Ok," and continued on his way. That company finished the job they were hired to do, and soon left the hospital. I was shocked to see him, but felt comfortable knowing that he had no idea where I lived...at least I thought that.

A couple of days later there was a knock on my door. I had become friends with my neighbors in the building, and they were the only ones who ever came to visit me, so I opened the door expecting one of them and found my husband standing there. Before I could speak, he forced his way into my apartment and shut the door. "How did you know where I live?" I asked him, feeling overwhelmed by the numerous amount of emotions I was experiencing at the time. "I followed you home," he said. "You got any money?" "No, I don't," I hollered "I don't want you here, and you need to leave now." He was able to grab hold of me and push me to the floor. He straddled me and pinned my arms to the floor with his knees, then began going through the pockets of my jeans. He found $50.00 that was neatly folded in my right front pocket, then glared at me and asked, "Why did you lie to me? You're going to pay for this." He then slapped me across my face and drug me to the bedroom and locked me in because he was afraid that I would kill him while he slept. *("How did he lock you in?" you may be asking. Well, the people that lived in the apartment before me had lots of animals...mainly snakes. They kept the snakes in the bedroom, so there was a latch installed on the outside of the door to padlock the room. When I first moved in and was cleaning, I found a snake in the kitchen and very calmly caught it and took it over to management and explained that there was a snake in my apartment. They were shocked to see a woman catch a snake and bring it to them without being hysterical, but I was also very adamant about them sending someone into the apartment and doing a thorough search through the whole place to guarantee there were no more surprises lurking anywhere.)*

So, needless to say, I was once again a prisoner in my own home. He never left the place and had shown up with his clothes in bags. He knew when my paydays were and if he did leave, he was always back by the time I came home from work...meaning, when he left, my apartment was left unlocked. This definitely did not sit well with me, and I had to find a way to get rid of him...quickly. Payday came, he wanted money, I refused to give it to him, we fought, he gained control, and took the money. Except, this time, I was extremely angry and fought so hard against him that I tore muscles in my right shoulder and was in excruciating pain. I knew I had to do something or I was not going to make it out alive this time. I needed help.

The next morning, I walked into my supervisor's office and asked to speak with her. She closed her door, and I began to tell her what was going on. Of course she asked, "When you first saw him, why didn't you say something to me?" "Because I felt that I could take care of myself and handle this on my own," I said. As we continued to talk, I began to cry and she began to cry with me. "Here is what we are going to do," she said. "I want you to go down to the emergency room and let them check you out. I will handle your medical records so nobody else will see them but me. While you're there, I will call and find out what can be done to get him removed from your apartment...I will have that information for you when you get back. It's going to be ok." Sitting in the

emergency room, I began to beat myself up again for letting this happen. "How

can I continue to be this stupid?" I kept asking myself. As the doctor began to

check out the injury, I cried out in pain as he tried to be as gentle as he could

possibly be. "Looks like you have some torn muscles and ligaments," he said.

"This will take a little while to heal. I'm going to give you some muscle relaxers

and you're going to have to keep your right arm and shoulder in a sling for a few

weeks so it can heal." I returned to my supervisor's office and explained to her

what the doctor had said. She then explained what I needed to do to get my

husband out of my apartment and advised me to take care of it as soon as

possible.

She had given me the rest of the day off, so I caught a bus to go downtown

and establish an Ex Parte order against him, which pretty much was a temporary

restraint order. I had a picture of him in my purse, which I voluntarily

surrendered for ID purposes. I knew he would be home waiting for me and

cringed at the thought that I would have to deal with him for another couple of

days before the Ex Parte kicked in. The bus ride back was a long one.

As I walked through the door, he looked up and wanted to know what had happened to my arm. Angrily I snapped back at him, "How dare you ask me what happened to me! You did this to me last night!" "I was only playing with you…I didn't realize I was that rough…Sorry," he said. He then noticed the brightly colored goldenrod paper I was holding which was my copy of the Ex Parte Order. "What's that?" he asked. As I nervously explained to him what it was, he became extremely upset and claimed that he wasn't going anywhere. Once again, I was shoved into the bedroom and locked in. I had to bang on the door for him to let me out to go to the bathroom, and he made sure that when I finished, I went right back to the bedroom. It was also very difficult getting ready for work the next couple of days as he watched me like a hawk…scared that at any moment, I would grab some sort of weapon and kill him. But, my justice came after a couple of days.

It was very early in the morning, and I, as usual, was locked in my bedroom. At around 2:00 am, he came into the room and woke me up. "The sheriff is outside and wants to talk to you," he abruptly said. Quickly I threw on adequate clothing and stepped outside the apartment door. "You recently obtained and Ex Parte order against this man," the deputy stated as he pulled out the picture I had provided. "Is the person in there now this person?" "Yes," I replied. "Do you still wish to carry out this order?" the deputy questioned. "Yes I do, please get him out of my apartment!" I replied. He then proceeded to advise me that if I allowed my husband back into the apartment after this, there would be nothing they could do to help me. I nodded in agreement. The deputy sheriffs then walked into the apartment and commanded him out. He tried to play on their sympathy saying, "But, I have nowhere to go, and I'll have to come back and get my clothes." "Not our problem," one of the deputies said, "you have to go now. You will not be allowed back into this apartment to get the rest of your belongings without being accompanied by a police officer...do you understand?" He nodded and began to try to make me feel guilty by crying out, "How could you do this to me? How could you just throw me out in the middle of the night like this? Why can't you let me stay until the morning?" The Deputies continued to force him out of the apartment and off the premises. He asked if he could come back and pick up the rest of his belongings if he brought along one of the pastors whose church he had attended in the past. I approved of the escort he had selected, so he came by and retrieved the rest of his things. I was now completely free. He's gone for good! The dark clouds have given way to bright sunshine. I'm flying, baby, flying!

## Chapter 15 – The Journey Forward

I had gained my freedom.  Now I could breathe…oh the relief of being able

to be myself again.  I can't exactly remember how it happened, but one day, I

believe, I was waiting for a bus to go somewhere when a gentleman offered me a

ride.  Normally I don't make it a practice to just get into cars with strangers, but

this one was different.  He began talking about his church, his wife, and his family.

He then began to tell me how he was involved with the community programming

station at the cable TV company, and how he learned how to run the cameras,

control the audio and graphics, and even direct.  I decided to tag along for the

ride…it was a ride that I was happy to take.  For the next couple of years, I learned

about television production, and was capable of handling the cameras,

teleprompters, audio, character generator graphics (typing in and automating the

beginning and ending credits on shows as well as naming guest during the show),

technical directing, and talent coordinating (placing microphones on the host and

guests, and seating them appropriately).  Eventually I ended up directing a few

live shows which really gave me quite an experience.

From the humble beginning, this gentleman, his family, and I developed

quite a relationship.  I began to attend the same church they did, and their children all became very fond of me.  As I began to open up and reveal what I had been through, they decided to "set me up" with one of their good friends.  According to them, he was a really sweet individual and was a great match for me.  Of course, after going through what I had gone through, I was very skeptical about anyone who even approached me about dating, but based on their assessment of him, I decided to give it a try.  I gave them my phone number which they forwarded to him, and he called the next day to set up a date.

The date was very nice.  Mark was the perfect gentleman...he opened the car door or business doors for me (in matter of fact, he made it a point to remind me every time I attempted to grab for a door handle), the conversation was very comfortable, and nothing that was discussed felt awkward.  We saw a movie, and afterwards, he took me home.  It was a very nice evening for me, and I felt everything went extremely well.  But, after a couple of days, he wouldn't answer my calls or return them.  He stopped coming by to see me, and I was beginning to become concerned that I had done something wrong.   My friends had invited me over to dinner after church one Sunday, and asked, "Have you spoken with Mark?"  I answered, "No, I haven't.  I have tried to call him...he won't answer.  I have left messages...he won't return my calls.  I hope I haven't done anything to run him away from me."  They looked at each other, then they both looked at me.

"We're so sorry, Brenda" they said. "We can't believe he hasn't spoken to you, and he should be telling you this…not us. Mark is marrying someone else in a week." My heart sank like a concrete brick falling to the bottom of the ocean. I could feel all the pain and hurt rising up inside of me, and it was just waiting to jump out of me like the roar of a lion. But all I could get out was a heavy sob. I broke down and cried for what seemed like an eternity, and everyone, including the children, surrounded me and placed their arms around me. The warmth of their love seemed to melt away all the abandonment I was feeling at that moment.

I went back home that evening to my lonely apartment, and began to frantically search for anything on the television set that would take my mind off of everything when the phone rang. Could it be Mark calling to say he was sorry for how he had treated me? I rushed over and picked up the phone…but it wasn't Mark…it was…my ex-husband. I had forgotten that he still had my phone number. Blatantly I asked, "What do you want?" "Oh…I just wanted to inform you that I was tested today for AIDS and I tested positive. So you have it now. You're going to die, and no other man in this world is going to want to have anything to do with you!" he said, then very abruptly hung up. Once again my heart sank. "Lord, how much more can I take of this?" I asked as I fell down on my knees. Fear struck all the way through my body. "I'm going to die," I thought to myself. Then something clicked. With having had to go through the emergency room with the injuries sustained from his last attack, the hospital had run blood and urine tests on me; checking for everything. All results had come back clear. He was lying to me. How could someone be so cruel and hateful to call and lie to another person like that, knowing the emotional distress it would put them through? I was now livid...as angry as any woman in my position could get. I took several deep breaths, and thanked God for reminding me about the tests the hospital had done, and slept soundly that night.

He had the nerve to call again the next day and admit that he had lied to me. At that point, it took every ounce of strength in my body not to jump through the phone and strangle the living mess out of him. I composed myself and said, "You know what? You have confused and tortured me for the last time. If you call me one more time, I will have you arrested for harassment. Do you understand me?" He hung up on me. My next step was to call the phone company and have my number changed. Now I wouldn't have to hear from him ever again.

I had dated several other people during the next few months, some of them I had no business even being involved with, but I needed the attention, I needed the affection; emotionally and physically. While it satisfied part of my longing, something was still missing. I wasn't happy with what I had, I wanted more…I wanted someone who just didn't want me for my money or sex, I wanted someone who wanted me for me. Was that too much to ask for?

## Chapter 16 – The Light at the End of the Tunnel

One year later, in 1990, the same scenario presented itself again. I was waiting for a bus to go to the television studio, when someone pulled over and asked if I needed a ride. Once again, I was very leery about getting into the car with a stranger, but this one was very different. He actually wanted to go to the studio with me to see what I did. His name...Mark *(No, this wasn't the same Mark that had just abandoned me. People named Mark were being placed in my life at that time for some reason)*. He was pretty interested in what I did, and eventually decided to volunteer as well in the studio. And, he didn't leave after one date. Sometimes he would pick me up from work and take me home...even though I lived 5 minutes away. Other times, he would pick me up and take me out to dinner. This guy was a keeper. We dated for 5 years, and had discussed marriage several times; or at least I did. He supported me through job changes, and 3 residential moves, which I thought was terrific. The change came when I made the move to Independence, MO. He lived in Kansas City, MO. I had noticed that Mark, had stopped visiting as much as he used to. My job had sent me to a training class in Fort Worth, TX for 3 days, so Mark had to come to Independence each day to make sure my little pug, Samson, went out to use the restroom and was fed. Once I came back, he picked me up at the airport, took me out to breakfast, then back to the apartment. It was then that the truth was revealed. "I'm sure you've noticed that I haven't been out to visit you very much lately. I need to talk to you about that," Mark said. "I've had trouble coming out here every day to take care of your dog. It's too much for me to drive out here, so if you want me to visit you more, you need to move back into Kansas City." I had just moved out to Independence, and now he wants me to move back to Kansas City? Now that was a surprise to me since it wasn't an issue before. There were other things I knew that I needed to change, and that was not a problem. The last straw was when he had picked me up, and we went to visit his mother. We walked in, then he said I have to make a run, I'll see you when I get back...he didn't come back for at least 6 hours. His mother, when he left, said, "Don't let him do that to you." I didn't know what else to do. I had talked until my face was blue, I had even helped with the "baby mama" issues that were going on in regards to his daughter. Many times I had taken my money to help purchase Christmas presents and clothes for her, so I felt that I had gone above and beyond what I needed to do because I did it from my heart. It wasn't long after this that Mark said, "I was hoping you could see what is happening...even Stevie Wonder could see it. I have found someone else, and I've been thinking about marrying her in the near future." Wow...slap in the face again. Is there something I'm doing wrong, or do I just need to stop dating men named Mark? Once again I'm

dumped, and not just for someone else, but marriage is in the picture. "During

our 5 years of dating we had talked about marriage, and now it was happening

with someone else!" I thought. At that point I was through with men. At the age

of 35, I didn't care if I never got married, or if I never had children. This process

was too painful for me to keep going through, and I couldn't take it anymore.

I picked myself up and carried on...like I usually did after a disaster. It was

1995, and I no longer had transportation to work, so I had to resort to riding the

bus to and from work each day. In the course of my daily bus ride, I made many

friends along the way. One of them was named Gail. At the time she was

pregnant with twins, and she always sat with me for the long ride. We began

talking about relationships, and I opened up about what had just happened to

me. She said, "I have the perfect guy for you. He works with me, he's in the

military, and he's a really great guy. You both would be perfect for each other.

"Oh, no" I thought. "I've had one bad experience with blind dates, and I'm not

going through this again!" But Gail kept pressing the issue day after day. Finally I

gave in and said "Ok, let's give it a try." I gave her my number to give to him. She

said, "His name is C.L. and he's a great guy. I have played match maker for 5

couples and none of them have divorced!" The comfort level raised very little with that statement, but nevertheless, either this was going to work, or I'd end up like always...alone. C.L. called me that night, and surprisingly, we talked for about 5 hours. I found out that he was in the Navy reserves, and lived with his sister (which I found out later, that I worked with her at a microfilming company that I used to work for.) We talked for days, then finally met each other. The chemistry was there, and we got along very well.

It wasn't long before I decide to move back to Kansas City, MO because of the living conditions at the residence I was at. C.L. and I moved in together and stayed in a 2 bedroom apartment for about 2 years. Eventually, he was able to buy a car, then later bought a house. This man knew what he wanted and knew how to get it. Somehow, I knew C.L. was the one that God had placed in my life. This was confirmed in 2008 as we exchanged our vows in marriage. The light at the end of the tunnel had overtaken me. I had finally found happiness, and it wasn't in the man, it was in the love that I felt, and the peace and comfort I felt. Finally I was home!

## Chapter 17 - Crisis in Paradise

Paradise...I had found paradise. The marriage was going well; C.L. had a great job, I had a great job, all our needs were met, and there was no trouble in sight...so I thought. The first four to five years were awesome. Then came the death of his Grandma Christian. This brought him a lot of heartache and grief. Shortly thereafter came the death of several of his great aunts and uncles who were the patriarchs of the family, then came the death of his own mother. The weight of it became so much that he shut himself off and would not talk to anyone; not me, not family, not our pastor...nobody. Our marriage began to suffer horrifically. I tried everything in my power to get his attention and some conversation, but it all fell on deaf ears and was met with anger or hostility. I had been working temporary jobs and had just been hired permanently by a manufacturing company doing Accounts Receivables and Collections, which I loved doing. There happened to be a young man there about my age, who after a week or two of me working there had struck up quite a conversation. Eventually, I opened up about the issues that were taking place in my marriage, and he began to provide suggestions and ideas regarding what C.L. may have been feeling or going through. I thought this was unusual...another man, who was not a pastor, trying to help me fix the problems with my husband. That attitude and concern drew me to him, and after a few months of trying every avenue possible, the marriage was not getting any better. As it began to fall apart, my new found friend was there to comfort and support me, and I found myself beginning to direct all my emotions and feelings towards him; regardless of the legal issues he was already dealing with *(He was on house arrest for various charges, and could only go to work/church and back home).* I begged for C.L. to talk to me; to just say "Hello, how are you?" But, that was not happening. So one thing led to another, and soon I found myself in a position that I did not want to be...I was having an affair. He soon found out about it, and things became very rocky to say the least. We talked about it, but he never forgave me for it.

This went on for years until finally, I could take it no more. I had prayed about it, and was given an answer that I was not ready for...separation. In despair I told him, "C.L., I can't do this anymore. I love you, but right now, I'm in the way of God working with you. I have to remove myself from this marriage so that you can figure out what is wrong." His answer was simply, "Do what you have to do!"

I moved in a building with a long-time friend of mine in Kansas. This building had been converted into rooms that were rented out and had 1 apartment that included a kitchen, living room, and bedroom. The bathroom was shared. So, in my pain, I agreed to move into the apartment and try to pull myself together. But, after several months, I found that even friends at times can get enough of each other. So, once again, I packed up everything I had, and found an apartment in Independence, MO. C.L. and I had promised to keep the lines of communication open with each other. We talked frequently about what was going on in our lives, our struggles, and the issue at hand. I figured that line of communication is what would bring us back together again...and it was.

## Chapter 18 – It All Ends

After being separated for 2 years, C.L. had figured out what his issue was. Having a stepmother, as a child, had its disadvantages, and it seemed that both he and his sister had suffered unfair treatment at the hand of their stepmother. So C.L. instead of basking in the accomplishments that he had made his whole life...car, new home, 15 years in the military, he had done everything to prove to everyone that he could do it. It really broke my heart when I found out he married me just to prove to everyone that he could do it. He did not understand what true love was, and was incapable of giving it. As hurt as I was, I knew he needed help, and I was going to be the one to help him through this. After all, I married him for better and for worse. In April of 2009, I moved back into the house with him, and began to try to help him mend. I also had a separate apartment as a "get away" when I needed to study for my classes and Bible College and establish my curriculum for the classes I was teaching. The apartment was a quiet solitude place where I could concentrate...the house, on the other hand, was always noisy. C.L. was always trying to fix something on the house, or had the television going 24 hours a day. We had begun to get closer, and C.L. had entered into a training program at the church we attended called the Stephens Ministry, which offered counseling to anyone who needed it. He completed the training and was commissioned as a Stephen Minister, and I could not have been any prouder of him. Everything was looking promising but the inevitable happened.

We still slept in separate bedrooms, so every morning, I would stop by his bedroom, tell him goodbye, and kiss him on his forehead before I left for work. I noticed that it was harder to get him to wake up. But, given the fact that he had diabetes, high cholesterol, and hypertension, and he had stopped taking the medication for all of them, I knew it was affecting him in that way. He had nosebleeds that would not seem to stop. We had talked about placing him on my health insurance from my job, but with him being a veteran, I thought it would be best for him to get his insurance through the Veterans Administration. As time passed, it did not seem that the VA was moving, so in November of 2009, I changed my insurance to add him to it.

I was looking forward to Christmas...our first Christmas back together after the separation, and was planning what to get him as gifts. One night at midnight, I heard noises in the attic which sounded like someone dropping dead weights. I immediate got up, walked to C.L.'s bedroom, woke him up and said, "Did you hear that?" "Hear what?" he said. "It sounds like someone is up in the attic dropping things." "It's nothing, go back to sleep," he groggily replied. I went back to lie down, when 20 minutes later, I heard the noise again. Once again, I woke him up, "I heard it again…there's something in attic!" Half sleep, he mumbled something and went back to sleep. "I know I'm not hearing things," I told myself as I headed back to my bedroom. As I was just getting settled in again, I heard the doorknob of the attic door jiggle. Now, this scared me. I ran and frantically woke him up and said, "Now something is jiggling the doorknob…you need to check and see what it is." "It's probably an animal," he said. "I'll take care of it tomorrow! Now go to bed," he snarled. Startled, scared, and a little angry, I slowly crept back to my bedroom to lie down, then…there came the sound of something being dropped again. I sat straight up in bed, clapped my hands once, and said, "In the name of Jesus, I command you to leave this place!" Immediately the noises stopped.

The next day, C.L. went up into the attic and took care of the problem like he usually did for any critter that invaded our home…he bombarded the attic with cayenne pepper. I laughed when he first shared

that deterrence with me, but nothing ever came back.

Two days later was December 10th. There was nothing unusual about

this day. I cleaned up, got dressed for work, and went through my usual

goodbye ritual with C.L. I opened the door and said, "Good morning

sunshine, I'm off to work!" He didn't move. I repeated the phrase

again...still he did not move. I proceeded to walk over to the bed to wake

him up. As I touched him, I knew something was wrong...he was cold...very

cold. "C.L. wake up!" I began to holler. I shook him and he would not

move. "Honey, please wake up...Oh God no!" I cried as I realized that he

was no longer here on this earth with me. I called 911 and the dispatcher

at the other end of the line tried to calm me down to get the needed

information. I imagine between the crying and the screaming, it was

difficult for her to understand me. I called my Pastor, and he immediately

was on his way to the house. Soon a police officer showed up, went

upstairs to confirm that C.L. was deceased, then placed a call for an

ambulance. The officer then offered to make any calls to family for me as I

was in no shape at all to make them. The ambulance showed up, and the

EMT went upstairs to confirm his passing, and as she came down, instructed that the coroner's office needed to be contacted. As I sat there in the living room, I did not know where I was mentally. I was in shock, hurting, sad, angry, scared...what had just happened. I wanted to scream but could not. I wanted to cry, but could not.

My pastor finally showed up, and a couple of other friends from the church showed up shortly afterwards. As we sat there, I began to get angry, not at God, but at Satan for taking someone I loved away from me. I all of a sudden felt a surge of strength and power and was ready to take the enemy on. I, along with one of my friends from church, went up the stairs to C.L.'s bedroom to say goodbye to him before the coroner's office took him away. I still could not believe he was gone, and that he had left without saying goodbye to me, or even allowing me to say goodbye to him. This...made me very angry with him. But not as angry as I would become in the months that followed.

## <u>Chapter 19 – The Deceit</u>

The next few months were pure hell for me.  I remained at the house as long as I could, and when I couldn't handle it any longer, I stayed at the apartment.  I cried myself to sleep just about every night, and talked to C.L. all the time as if he were standing right in front of me.  About 2 weeks after he passed away, I had cried myself to sleep, and had a dream.  I dreamt that I was sitting in the living room, in the chair that was his favorite chair.  I was looking at the remote to turn on the television, and as I looked up, C.L. was standing right in front of me.  My heart leapt with joy at the sight of him, and I began crying as I muttered, "Hi C.L...how are you.  I've missed you so much...where are you?"  He, very chalantly looked at me and said, "Duh! I'm right here!"  At that point I woke up, but I felt so different.  I no longer was sad...I was no longer hurt.  It seemed like everything had just lifted off of me.  Somehow, I knew that he was ok, and that I didn't need to cry anymore.

I began to spend a lot of time on the internet.  Not necessarily looking for love, but looking for someone to talk to...someone to ease the loneliness a little, when all of a sudden someone instant messaged me.  He said he wanted to talk to me because he was looking for someone to talk to as well.

"What's the harm in it?" I thought to myself, so we struck up a conversation. Days turned into weeks, and weeks into months. This man said that he was stationed at Base Balad in Iraq. He was divorced with 2 kids and was from Kentucky. He sent pictures of himself, especially of him in Iraq. He also sent pictures of his uniform. There were subtle signs that something was wrong, but I was lonely so much, that I was willing to overlook them. As time went on, the conversation began to change, and he began to tell me how much he would like to meet me and spend time with me. He asked for my address so that he could send me flowers for my birthday, which he did…18 beautiful long-stem roses. They were the most beautiful roses I had ever seen. He talked about coming home and retiring from the military and spending time with me. Once again, there were signs…the misspelling of simple words and the grammar errors in his instant messages, the change in gender tenses in the conversations sometimes, and at times, it seemed like he was having a conversation with someone else because the subject would change in mid-conversation, but still I overlooked them.

Then came the requests for money to get him a satellite phone, to help him get food, and finally to help get him back here to the US to see me. At first I struggled with it, but he was able to talk me into it. I couldn't get the address out of him to send him a card, so I looked up the address on a military site, and came across a warning about internet scamming. I mentioned it to him, which upset him to no end. (*I guess I would be upset too if someone was accusing me of being a scammer when I was trying to establish a relationship!*) So, once again, I ignored the warning signs. Associates that I had who had been in the military warned me against sending money, and even provided the options he had...still, I did not listen. I went online to lookup something else, and there was the warning again regarding internet scamming. This time, I read through the whole thing...my heart sank. All the signs listed matched what this man had been doing. I immediately began questioning him on all sorts of things. I did my research on his division in the Army, and began asking him questions about the leadership and the history of it. He kept signing out of instant messaging, which I later discovered was his way of finding the answer, and when he logged back on, he would provide the answer. Of course, the excuse for the logouts, according to him, had something to do with the internet connections in Iraq! I had discovered that the emails he had sent were not coming from Iraq as he had claimed, but from Nigeria. These people scammed me for 4 months, and I let them. I was crushed beyond repair. First I lose my husband of 11 years, and now someone plays on my emotions, and scams me. At this point, I was through with communicating on the internet, and through with men. I had been hurt way too many times, and I was not going to be hurt again...by anyone. Thankfully, I was able to find a support group that dealt specifically with people who had been romantically scammed, and they saved my life. Now, to get back on my feet, do damage control, and get my finances back in order. That was going to be a challenge, but God finally smacked me in the face to wake me up, and I was hearing him clear as a bell now. "What's Next Lord?"

## Chapter 20 – Finally...Happiness

By now, I had finally determined that God wanted me to be alone. Every relationship I had entered into had ended tragically, and I was growing increasingly tired of being hurt and abused.  I had enough of being taken advantage of, and I was not going to let this happen again.  I began to remove myself from all internet dating sites...even a Christian dating site that I had become involved with did not seem like a Christian dating site. Relationships were becoming the farthest thing from my mind now, and all I wanted to do was become as close as I could to God.  He was the only one that had not hurt me, or deceived me, and he was the only one that I could depend on and trust.

As I began to close my account on the last dating site, I saw that someone had expressed interest in me.  "Nope, we're not going that route again," I thought to myself, but there was a tugging at my heart to dig a little further and find out about this person.  I juggled the thought back and forth for a while before clicking to see what this interested person wanted. As I began to read the bio, I noticed the familiar misspelled words and phrases that were the sure sign of a scammer.  There were no pictures, so I could not even see what this person looked like. Red flags began to rise, and my heart began to beat quickly. As I began to exit out of the bio, I felt the tug again. "Lord, is this you, or is this my emotions running amuck again?" I questioned myself. I decided I would reply to see what the response would be, so I quickly typed a note to ask for a picture. Unfortunately, his response was, "I don't know how to upload pictures on here...I'm sorry. If I knew how I would." Hmmm, the scammer said that he couldn't turn his computer camera on because of military regulations...similar scenarios. I continued the observations and asked where he lived, how long he lived there, and how old he was. Everything he responded with matched what was listed on his bio on the site, but I still was not sure about this person. He continued the online conversation and provided his phone number for me to call him if I wanted to...it was a local Missouri number. "Ok," I thought, "At least this person is nearby, and the phone number proves it." He had said that he was Caucasian, which I had no problem with, and he knew that I was African American, which he had no problem with. I hesitantly gave him a call, and was instantly mistaken for someone else he had an unpleasant experience with, but he quickly realized who I was, and immediately apologized for the mishap. We began to talk, and I began to feel a little more "at ease."

After about 1 hour of talking, he decided to ask me out for dinner that night. Of course, I was not going to invite him to my place, so we decided on a barbecue joint to eat. I nervously and eagerly waited for him outside my apartment building to pick me up, and when he arrived, I was not disappointed. Out stepped this 5 foot 9, silver haired, blue-eyed, strapping man. He was very polite and kind; even opening the car door for me, which I had not seen in years. As we drove to the eating place, we engaged in small talk and attempted to find out more about each other. As we walked into the restaurant, he held the door open for me, and I was already beginning to like this guy. As we sat and ate our food, I caught him several times just staring at me, which unnerved me a little. He noticed it, and said, "Oh, I'm sorry for staring...it's just that I can't believe how beautiful you are. You are the most beautiful woman I have ever seen!" My heart just melted. Out of all the relationships I had been involved in, this was the first man that actually told me I was beautiful.

The drive back home was very pleasant indeed. There was a "Look-out" site just up the street from where I lived, and at night, you could see the blue and red runway lights of a small airport that was close by, the mighty Missouri River, Interstate 70, and a beautiful view of a bridge that was lit up with red lights as traffic crossed it travelling north and southbound. There was a light cool breeze blowing that cooled the hotness of the passing day. As we stood looking at the beauty, he placed his arm around me. "Do I tell him to remove his arm, do I remove it, or do I allow this?" I questioned myself again. I decided to allow it. "Yep," he said, "You're going to be my wife!" "Wait a minute, you don't know me, and I don't know you. Don't you think it's way too soon to even be thinking about this?" I said, with the whole scammer ordeal still fresh on my mind. "You're right, I'm sorry" he apologetically said. We continued talking more throughout the coming weeks. He would call me every day when he came home from work; no matter how tired he was, he would call and talk to me until he couldn't stay awake any longer. I picked up lunch one Sunday afternoon after church, and decided to take it over to his place. We had a wonderful brunch as he began to open up a little more about his life. He revealed how that he had a hearing problem, and that he had to learn sign language which he now fluently knew. He even went as far as to sign a couple of songs to me as he played them on his cassette player. As I sat and listened, I watched him sign each word and phrase of the song with emotion and feeling. As he finished the last song, the Holy Spirit began to speak to my heart, and I heard that familiar small, still voice speak and say, "Pray for him." I obediently asked him, "Would you mind if I prayed for you?" "No, please do," he said. I began praying for him. Following the direction of the Holy Spirit, I placed my hands on both of his ears, and began praying for his hearing to be restored and healing of the nerve damage done because of the deterioration of the eardrums. As I prayed, he began to weep emotionally, and I could feel the hurt and pain that he had been carrying around with him. When I finished praying, he said, "I felt a "pop" in my ears, and I can hear a little better. Thank you so much!" I just wanted him to know who I lived for, and that there was power and grace sufficient enough to make possible all that seemed impossible.

After a short period of time, I met his family. I was a little concerned about what they would think of me because of my race, but they received me and accepted me. We had dated for 5 months, and now it was Thanksgiving. I had decided that I wanted to cook dinner, so I cooked a majority of things to take over to his mom's house to celebrate Thanksgiving with his mom, brother, aunt, uncle, and grandma. He had cooked the turkey, and I had cooked brisket, oyster dressing, greens, and peach cobbler. Everyone ate until they were full, and I enjoyed the time spent with him and his family. It was following dinner that was magical. I love jewelry, so wherever it is available, I window shop. It was that night that he proposed to me. I knew the possibility was there...I just did not think it would be that soon. The ring was absolutely gorgeous. It was so delicate, but it looked like it was created just for me. Of course I said "Yes" which made him the happiest person in the world.

He wanted to get married on June 5th, which was the day we met and our first date, but that date in the following year fell on a Sunday, so we opted for June 4th. Those 7 months went by quickly, and my best friend in the world, Sarah, drove all the way to Independence, MO from Colorado to be my matron of honor. I was so excited and happy to have her with me to share this special time. This was my third marriage, and I was determined that if this one did not work, I was never getting married again, and it would only be God and me for the rest of my life...period!

Wedding day was full of the normal bridal jitters. The cake was being delivered that day, all the refreshments had to be placed on ice to chill, the usual nuts and mints had to be placed in the bowls, etc. Earlier that morning, Sarah had decided to take professional pictures of me in my wedding gown in the park across from where I lived. The morning sun cast a warm glow across the trees and the old stone gazebo in the park, and Sarah took advantage of that beauty and placed me in the midst of it. I offered to pay her for services, but she suggested it was a wedding gift to me. All of this was done without my husband-to-be knowing about it...he was going to have a surprise wedding gift.

As I was getting ready to walk down the aisle, Sarah ran back to me and asked "Where are the rings?" Horror struck me as I realized that I had left our wedding bands at home...still in the boxes they came in. Panic started to set in and I could begin to feel my breath being sucked out of me. I struggled to fight back the tears as I realized I had forgotten the most important things. Immediately efforts were made to calm me down, the bridal march was playing, and I needed to make an appearance. Two people offered rings for us to use in the ceremony, and the wedding took place. In the middle of the ceremony, we had chosen a song to be played before we said our vows.  During the song, my husband-to-be asked,

"Where are the rings?"  Fighting back tears, I answered, "I'm sorry...I forgot

and left them at home.  Are you mad at me?"  He smiled and answered,

"No, I love you."  That day, I left as Mrs. William N. Craven Jr.  It was a very

happy day for me.

The following months brought numerous challenges.  William, which

everyone calls him by his nickname, Bill, began experiencing pain in his

shoulders and wrists.  His fingers locked up at times, and he was

experiencing pain in his heels as well.  This caused him to lose his job

shortly after we were married, and I soon found myself "holding the fort

down" all alone.  Two years have passed, and now it is him that is bearing

the brunt of the responsibility, but it is a positive situation.  You see, I was

able to go into full time ministry.  Everything I had gone through in my life,

was to get me to this point.  All the hurt, the pain, the struggles, the

bruises, the cuts, the abrasions...all the battle scars are there to prove that I

went through the battles, survived, and healed.  I thought my calling was to

be an evangelist, to go out and spread God's word, and to spiritually

call/bring order back to places that had lost it.  That responsibility is still

there, but there was something else God wanted me to do.  He wanted me to use my experiences to help others who have gone through, or who are going through what I went through.  Especially pastors and lay people who deal with the everyday issues of their parishioners, then feel there is nowhere to turn when they need help.  God was calling me to be a counselor.  I was blessed to obtain my Doctorate in Evangelism with an emphasis in healing and deliverance in 2012, and my Doctorate in Scriptural Psychology with an emphasis in teaching and research in 2013 from Faith Bible College in Independence, MO.

As I've told this story, many have said, "Oh, I am so sorry that you had to go through this.  I don't know how you did it!"  The answer is: *I had to go through it to get where I am today.  Many of the situations I experienced were due to my disobedience and rebellion against God and the Holy Spirit.  Those were learning experiences for me.  I grew through them, I became a stronger woman in God through them.  I gained strength, power, and wisdom through them.  Some situations were times when God allowed me to be tested.  I have accepted them all, and will accept any other tests that God sends my way.  "Why open the door for trials and tribulations you may ask?"* **James 1:2-3 says, "My brethren, count it all joy when ye fall into divers temptations; knowing this, that the trying of your faith**

**worketh patience.** *Verse 4 continues on stating that we should allow patience to have her perfect work, that we would be perfect and complete; wanting nothing. The moral of this is not to try to handle everything and fix the problem on our own, but to step back and let God do what he does best...turn the impossible into the possible; moving and only taking steps when he instructs and directs us to do so in wisdom. When there's abuse, poverty, and abandonment, times are difficult. It is painful, harsh, and even sometimes life-threatening. But the God of creation knows your heart, he knows you better than anyone else in the world...He created you. And, he loves you much more than any person could ever love another. He loves you so much, that he sent his Son, Jesus, to die for your sins well over 2,000 years ago, so that you would not have to pay the penalty of eternal damnation. Jesus paid that price for you. All you have to do is accept him as your Lord and Savior, and allow him to take full control of your life and destiny. It's a very simple process...just simply say this prayer:*

*Lord Jesus, I am a sinner. I have tried to do things my way, but Lord, I realize that I need to surrender to you. You said that no man comes to the father but by you. You are the way, the truth, and the life. Lord Jesus, I believe that you were born of the Virgin Mary, that you lived, died, were buried, and that you rose again on the third day for my freedom. I believe that your shed blood had freed me from the clutches of the Devil and that now I'm free to live a life of victory for you, and I believe your very words that I will not perish but have eternal life according to what you said in John 3:16. Lord, I thank you that I am now saved, and that I am bound for Heaven one day to be with you. In your name I pray...Amen.*

If you prayed that prayer, I welcome you with open arms into the family of God. You have just gained millions of brothers and sisters in the world who have been, are, and will be praying for you on a daily basis...around the clock. It is not by coincidence that you have picked up this book to read it. I was wrongly treated for many years, but my message to you is to not to get stuck living in the past and allowing the memories, hurt and pain to hold you captive. Instead, allow them to catapult you into a new life...one of overcoming, victory, peace and love. Allow your past experiences to become, **"A BLESSING IN DISGUISE!"**